"Polarization is one of the gravest illnesses infecting the US Catholic Church. In fact, Catholics often have an easier time talking with members of other Christian denominations and other religious traditions than with one another. Before we can accomplish anything in our church, we must first be able to talk to one another charitably. This book is an important step forward, as some of the church's most thoughtful men and women lay out the scope of the problem, consider its roots, and point to healthy and life-giving ways to move ahead. Essential reading for Catholics in the United States."

—James Martin, SJ
Author of *Jesus: A Pilgrimage*

"The volume is a rich collection of essays that offer a diversity of voices on the reality of polarization in the Catholic Church, a polarization that reflects the reality of the broader American reality. The essays offer wisdom drawn from personal experiences of polarization brought to bear on the expertise of religious leaders, academics, and advocates. I encourage anyone interested not only in understanding the phenomenon of polarization in the Church but also in finding insights into strategies to address it to pick up this book. The honest assessments of the wounds in our Church and society are coupled with genuine hope for healing grounded in the various authors' experiences of working toward creating the space for genuine dialogue. This volume is a gift to those of us who long to help create such spaces. It was truly a pleasure to read this work. I intend to bring different essays into my various classes, work with students, and conversations with colleagues."

—Catherine Punsalan-Manlimos, PhD
Malcolm and Mari Stamper Endowed Chair in Catholic
    Intellectual and Cultural Traditions
Director, Institute for Catholic Thought and Culture
Associate Professor, Theology and Religious Studies
Seattle University

"Pope Francis reminds us that 'open and fraternal debate makes theological and pastoral thought grow.' We should welcome such debate as evidence of a vibrant Church engaging issues at the heart of our faith. *Polarization in the US Catholic Church* advances this effort, challenging Catholics to remember that ours is a Church of relationship rooted in love and that our discourse must reflect that if we're to advance our evangelizing mission."

— Kim Daniels
Former spokesperson for the president of the
US Conference of Catholic Bishops

Polarization in the US Catholic Church

Naming the Wounds, Beginning to Heal

Edited by
Mary Ellen Konieczny,
Charles C. Camosy,
and Tricia C. Bruce

LITURGICAL PRESS
Collegeville, Minnesota

www.litpress.org

Cover design by Monica Bokinskie.

1	2	3	4	5	6	7	8	9

Library of Congress Cataloging-in-Publication Data

Names: Konieczny, Mary Ellen, editor.
Title: Polarization in the US Catholic Church : naming the wounds,
    beginning to heal / edited by Mary Ellen Konieczny, Charlie C. Camosy,
    and Tricia C. Bruce.
Description: Collegeville, Minnesota : Liturgical Press, 2016. | Includes
    bibliographical references.
Identifiers: LCCN 2016007173 (print) | LCCN 2016023779 (ebook) | ISBN
    9780814646656 (pbk.) | ISBN 9780814646908 (ebook)
Subjects: LCSH: Catholic Church—United States. | Conflict
    management—Religious aspects—Catholic Church.
Classification: LCC BX1406.3 .P65 2016 (print) | LCC BX1406.3 (ebook)
    | DDC 282/.7309051—dc23
LC record available at https://lccn.loc.gov/2016007173

Contents

Acknowledgments

This book comes directly from a conference of the same title held at the University of Notre Dame in April 2015. We want to begin by expressing our gratitude to the following sponsors.

The *Our Sunday Visitor* Institute and the Louisville Institute deserve special thanks. Both organizations not only helped to fund the conference but also supported the authors contributing to this book. We are grateful also to the following conference sponsors: The Henkels Lecture Fund, Notre Dame Institute for Scholarship in the Liberal Arts; the Notre Dame Center for Ethics and Culture; the Notre Dame Center for Social Concerns; the Notre Dame Center for the Study of Religion and Society; the Department of Sociology at the University of Notre Dame; the Notre Dame Cushwa Center for the Study of American Catholicism; and Fordham University's Center on Religion and Culture.

We must offer a special note of thanks to Michael McGillicuddy, whose insistence that Mary Ellen and Charlie have a meeting set in motion a series of events that led to the publishing of this book. Another debt of special thanks is due to Katie Camosy, Charlie's sister, who filmed and directed the production of a video from the conference—at a deep discount.

Thanks are definitely due Liturgical Press, which worked overtime to make sure this book came out on deadline. Hans Christoffersen and his staff kept us on track, happily, in the most painless ways possible. Charlie and Mary Ellen would like to single out our coeditor Tricia Bruce as well; without her efforts, this book would simply not have gone to press on time.

Finally, we are extremely grateful for the participation of Bishop Daniel Flores (Brownsville), Bishop Michael Mulvey (Corpus Christi), and Rev. John I. Jenkins, CSC, president of the University of Notre Dame. Thanks also to each of the delegates to the Notre Dame conference who were not formal contributors to this book; be assured that your interventions have helped to shape the following pages in profound ways.

Introduction

Polarization
in the US Catholic Church

Mary Ellen Konieczny

"I am a casualty of two culture war skirmishes—one in the '60s, the other in the '80s—and I have the scars to prove it. These scars have dogged me over the years. I have never shed the resentments I formed when my deepest beliefs and convictions were disparaged . . . and I have rarely felt safe enough to reengage on contested issues."

— Michael McGillicuddy, address to Polarization in the US Catholic Church conference, April 29, 2015

Universality—that is, small "c" catholicity—and, therefore, unity amid diversity are fundamental to Roman Catholicism. But in recent years, divisions around issues that are by now all too familiar—perhaps most notably, issues of gender, sexuality, and authority—have rent the Catholic Church in the United States. Divisions over these issues, of course, are not unique to Catholics. We live in a larger society in which divisiveness and vitriol are evident in many of the local churches of religious traditions practiced in the United States. These divisions are often produced in tandem with our public politics and, perhaps, paradigmatically reflected in them. And although conflict is not only sociologically necessary but also often a healthy part of societal interaction, these conflicts appear to be unproductive and intractable.

As a result, rather than the healthy debates characteristic of a living tradition, we have witnessed—in our churches, in our public politics, and in the local context of our everyday lives—an absence of genuine engagement and dialogue. Catholics of good will often feel alienated from one another. As described in the epigraph above, this alienation is not the product of a mere disagreement but of disrespect and dismissal of others. It wounds people. Cardinal Sean O'Malley has described the current climate of polarization as "a cancer in the Church." This is a disturbingly apt metaphor applied to the church as the Body of Christ. Moreover, it is no surprise that the issues provoking these debates are often described as "neuralgic," since they are not only long-standing and painful but also difficult to address much less heal.

So what are we, as Catholics and as citizens, to do? This was the question that emerged when Michael McGillicuddy first brought Professor Charles Camosy and me together to discuss cultural conflicts in church and society in the summer of 2013—a collaboration that led us to gather concerned colleagues and friends for a larger discussion and that has resulted ultimately in this edited volume.

The premise behind this book is one that, we believe, suggests a path toward answering the question of what to do. This premise is not new, of course. In our case, it owes a particular debt to the late Cardinal Joseph Bernardin of Chicago, in whose administration I worked and whose work to unify and heal American Catholics has grounded the work of many others. Although particular "hot button" issues—and the relational and emotional climate of debates surrounding them—have divided American Catholics, there is much that yet binds us together both as Catholics and as citizens. In fact, despite the magnified influence those at the poles of these debates can exert, sociological studies of polarization suggest that only a small minority of the population occupy truly polar positions on these controversial issues. Our goal in this book, therefore, is to better understand the social, emotional, and religious underpinnings of our divisions. With this context, we are better able to explore how what we *do* agree on—our common beliefs and aspirations—can help us heal the hurts our divisions have caused.

This book grew out of a conference about polarization in the Catholic Church with the same underpinnings, held at the University of Notre Dame on April 28 and 29, 2015. Camosy and I gathered nearly sixty Catholic pastors, public intellectuals, and professors—primarily theologians and social scientists—from across the United States. This group of people embodied widely different and often opposing views on divisive issues within the Catholic Church while also being committed to charity, listening, and engagement in dialogue. We included people of Vatican II and post–Vatican II Catholic generations as well as Millennial Catholics. We especially wanted younger, newer, and racially and ethnically diverse voices in the conversation. And we sought to offer a public platform to reach audiences beyond the academy.

The conference and this resulting volume, thus, bring new voices to the conversation. Contributors represent groups in different social locations than those most often engaged in debates around polarizing issues. Consequently, we reorient this debate by opening up new perspectives, avenues less well trod for traversing the landscape of cultural conflict among American Catholics.

We conceived the process of the conference through the "see-judge-act" model of Catholic Action, bringing both theological and social-scientific perspectives into the dialogue. We chose this method believing that if we began with a careful and informed observation and assessment of current cultural conflicts among Catholics and in society more broadly, we could then think creatively about small but concrete steps we might take toward promoting healing and a greater sense of unity among us. This book is one such step in this direction.

To introduce the chapters that follow, I will first briefly set the scene by providing a social-scientific answer to one of the first questions asked by participants on the second morning of the conference: "Exactly what do we mean by 'polarization'?" I then explore how reflecting on this question can help us understand what we observe in the cultural conflicts existing in church and society today. In this context, I briefly describe how the chapters proceed, through which we hope that readers will ultimately feel invited to "see, judge, and act" themselves.

What Is "Polarization"?

Open a dictionary to look for the words "polarize" or "polarization," and you'll typically find a definition originating in the hard sciences. Polarization describes light, radiation, or magnetism, where particles or forces move in opposite directions. But there is also a parallel, social definition. The Cambridge Dictionary, for example, defines it as "to cause something, especially something that contains different people or opinions, to divide into two completely opposing groups."[1] It is this latter definition that signals a growing experience of, and concern regarding, social polarization in contemporary societies.

This definition is a good representation of how social scientists understand polarization. Polarized attitudes describe a population comprised of two diametrically opposed positions. The two groups espousing sharply contrasting views are about equally split. In other words, like magnetic poles, polarized groups are opposed to each other and of equal strength. Methodologically, this strength is assessed numerically.

But if we look at American society, oddly enough, the definition mostly doesn't hold. The most recent social-science debates about polarization began in the late 1980s, with James Davison Hunter's book *Culture Wars*, which contended that the structure of public conflicts in the United States had become

---

[1] *Cambridge Dictionaries Online*, s.v. "polarize," accessed February 16, 2016, http://dictionary.cambridge.org/dictionary/english/polarize.

increasingly polarized.[2] Religion played a constitutive role in these conflicts, pitting traditionalists against progressives. According to Hunter, this polarization was evident in several kinds of debates, including those revolving around the family, education, law, art, and politics. But many now dispute this thesis. In fact, scholars have shown that the American public is *not* polarized on most issues. In general, survey research indicates that only between 10 and 20 percent of the American public hold polar positions around most "culture wars" issues. The majority hold more moderate positions. Over the last twenty years or so, only on the issues of abortion and same-sex marriage have researchers found that Americans are truly polarized—that is, that the population is about equally split and clustered at two contrasting poles of these debates.[3] From a social-science perspective, it is more accurate to speak of most of these issues as "cultural conflicts" in the public sphere, albeit highly public and potentially polarizing ones.

So why is it that many of us often feel like we live in a polarized society and church? There are a few different answers to this question, I think. Scholars—and perhaps our own observations of social life—tell us that the "culture wars" debates are waged largely by elites. Even casual observation suggests some of the ways in which elites help to create perceptions of a polarized populace, especially since media give the most time to attention-grabbing positions on issues. And in the current cultural climate, sharper positions closer to the poles attract more attention than moderation. The tenor of public debates

---

[2] James Davison Hunter, *Culture Wars: The Struggle to Define America* (New York: Basic Books, 1991).

[3] See Paul DiMaggio, John Evans, and Bethany Bryson, "Have Americans' Social Attitudes Become More Polarized?," *American Journal of Sociology* 102, no. 3 (November 1996): 690–755. See also Alan Wolfe, "The Culture War that Never Came," in *Is There a Culture War? A Dialogue on American Values and Public Life*, ed. James Davison Hunter and Alan Wolfe (Washington, DC: Brookings Institution and Pew Research Center, 2006), 67–84.

in American society has decreased in civility over the last few decades, and extreme statements are often rewarded with media time and attention.

In addition, there is clearly an emotional dimension involved in perceptions of polarization in American society generally and among ourselves as Catholics in particular. As McGillicuddy's remarks reveal, those who feel deeply about their faith can feel scarred by experiences of having their views disparaged. And when this happens, they can become disengaged. We see evidence of this in the recent growth of the number of "ex" or former Catholics.

The social theorist Georg Simmel can help us to understand why disagreements among people of faith may be so intense as to feel polarizing. He explains that antipathy is more intense among disagreeing people who belong to the same group, saying that "antagonism on the basis of a common kinship tie is stronger than that among strangers."[4] As a church, we often speak in familial images to explain our belonging. This expresses the intimacy involved in religious faith and has consequences for how we relate to one another. Simmel notes that this principle of social interaction is particularly true in churches, where he observes that even small differences can become sources of intense conflict.

Despite differences of class, race, and gender, we as Americans are held together by our many similarities—including, especially, our faith commitments, beliefs, and common sense of belonging—as well as the interpersonal ties we have with Catholic family members, friends, and people in our faith communities. Moreover, according to Simmel, the emotions evoked by the similarities and sense of belonging we share can be heightened when we have disagreements that are logically irreconcilable—even when these differences are relatively

---

[4] Georg Simmel, "Conflict," in *On Individuality and Social Forms*, ed. Donald N. Levine (Chicago: The University of Chicago Press), 70–95, here 90.

small. This, of course, is what we find when opposing views are framed as "all" or "nothing." In these situations, we may find ourselves at an impasse. In response, we might consider another of McGillicuddy's observations. He exhorts, "It's extremely challenging to 'get' those worldviews that most diverge from our own, yet we must summon the curiosity and humility to do so."[5] It seems to me that the authors of the chapters that follow have summoned these virtues in themselves and aim to pique Catholics' curiosity in describing how they attempt to engage worldviews other than their own.

Plan of the Book

In part 1, six prominent scholars, Catholic leaders, and public intellectuals reflect on how they see the problems and the promise of today's church from their own particular experiences and point of view. The first five of these brief reflections comprise chapter 1. They were initially presented as opening remarks during a plenary panel on the first evening of the conference. Most Reverend Daniel Flores, bishop of Brownsville, Texas, sees the wounds caused by divisions between Catholics as rooted in "the loss of confidence that the members of the household of the faith actually love one another" and advocates a renewal of charitable and familial relations within the church. Next, Reverend John I. Jenkins, CSC, draws on his experiences as president of the University of Notre Dame to ask and answer the question, "Why does the most caustic [criticism] come from sisters and brothers with whom I share a faith in Christ and am called, in the church, to build a civilization of love?" Then Christian ethicist Julie Hanlon Rubio considers polarization from the point of view of Catholics who are discouraged and disaffiliating, as well as from that of the most committed, concluding that we must talk about sex and gender to heal the church's wounds. She

---

[5] See Michael McGillicuddy's remarks in chap. 2 of this volume, p. 27.

sees the Synod on the Family as a crucial step in that direction. Sociologist Christian Smith follows in a related vein by noting that most Millennials' perspectives are quite different from those represented by polarizing debates within the church. Finally, Michael Sean Winters, columnist at the *National Catholic Reporter* and US correspondent for the *Tablet*, reminds us that ours is not the only age during which Catholics have waged battles and fiercely disagreed. The church, Winters asserts, needs both liberals and conservatives and "must be comfortable with, walk with, and learn from both kinds of people." The sixth of these brief reflections is presented in chapter 2. It is by Michael McGillicuddy, an active Catholic and a social worker in Chicago who, through his honesty, his earnest desire to take action, and his energy, inspired the conference and this book. He gave the opening remarks on the morning of the second day of the conference. He gives us, so to speak, the "view from the pew."

Parts 2 through 4 of this volume originated in the three sets of panel presentations that formed the basis of conference discussions on day two. In part 2, the authors address how cultural conflicts and polarizing public debates have been experienced among particular groups of Catholics and the resulting wounds that need healing. Chapters 3 and 4 present divergent parish perspectives. In chapter 3, sociologist Tricia Bruce examines the landscape of Catholic parishes, focusing her lens on what we can learn from personal parishes, where we see some groups who occupy positions close to the poles of cultural conflicts in the church. By contrast, Susan Crawford Sullivan, also a sociologist, discusses the everyday routines of many suburban Catholic parishes. Here we glimpse the perspectives and the needs of Catholics who do not seem to engage in, or run from, polarizing issues and public cultural conflicts. Theologian Brian Flanagan writes perceptively in chapter 5 about the challenges and pain experienced by gay and lesbian Catholics. In chapter 6, Holly Taylor Coolman describes how the college students in her courses come to them either ill-informed, misinformed, or both. They grapple with the church's teachings about marriage and sexuality, not knowing what the church offers. This generation, she observes, finds it difficult to imagine the possibility of a lifelong commitment when speaking about marriage. A polarized church, evident even in the much-needed Synod on the Family, only complicates this situation since, in polarizing discourses, people are presenting positions but not really engaging one another. These four chapters, then, give us a swath of viewpoints and an appreciation of the wounds people may experience, especially when they find themselves close to one pole of debate over issues that are presently controversial within American Catholicism.

The authors in part 3 assess the landscape of cultural conflicts in church and society through three different lenses. In chapter 7, Christian ethicist David Gushee argues from his personal religious history, which includes both evangelical Protestantism and Catholicism, together with the recent political history of US society, that Catholicism is uniquely equipped to resist polarization and present a hopeful sign for the future of the nation. Law professor Amy Uelmen speaks in chapter 8 from the perspective of her membership in the Focolare movement and her experience of teaching young adults, exploring how the "see-judge-act" model might be rethought to better promote authentic listening and direct discussions about polarizing issues. She sees Millennials as having particular strengths for these discussions, especially when given encouragement that claiming one's own positions need not imply the judgment of another's. And in chapter 9, theologian Nichole Flores makes the essential point that "neuralgic" church and cultural issues are not the only ones that can be polarizing. If we focus on them, we egregiously omit the role played by race in conflicts in US society. She uses current issues involving race, and student responses to them, to highlight how shared experience of rituals among those with different perspectives can create bonds and move people away from disengagement in conflict and toward empathy.

Part 4 of this volume looks to social groups who form the future basis of church and society. In chapter 10, journalist Elizabeth Tenety presents a moving account of the Millennial generation. She gives voice to how Millennial Catholics' life experiences while growing to adulthood, including 9/11 and the Great Recession, color their ways of thinking about American society, the Catholic Church, and cultural conflicts in the church. Erin Stoyell-Mulholland, also a Millennial Catholic and recent undergraduate at the University of Notre Dame, gives us another perspective on this generation's concerns and how we as a church might move forward through the lens of her participation in the pro-life movement. In chapter 12, theologian Hosffman Ospino discusses the central position Hispanics will occupy in the future of American Catholicism and how Hispanics' growing presence within the United States has the power to uniquely shape Catholics' concerns in ways that refocus energies positively, uniting them to address both material and spiritual needs. And in chapter 13, theologian Michael Peppard interrogates the relationship between polarization in American culture and politics and polarization among Catholics. The fact that Catholics fight one another so openly, he says, "is paradoxically a sign of Catholicism's general acceptance . . . in contemporary America." He advocates a series of concrete, practical suggestions for appreciating our diversity as Catholics and, at the same time, resisting further polarization among us.

We invite readers to journey with us through these pages, uniting friends, companions, and all who share their thoughts and experiences here. We hope you might join us in reflecting on how engaging those with different views on controversial issues might challenge each of us to revise and incorporate new understandings of the issues that divide us so as to bring healing and hope.

Engaging in dialogue about our differences as Catholics means facing the challenge of connecting differing communities of thought and practice. Those who take up this work are essentially engaging in what some call "translation" and others "bridging discourses." In this volume, Amy Uelmen describes something akin to bridging discourse as "a wide horizon for engagement" that "opens when we recognize that discussions are not only about identifying principles and values but also about the human drama, the challenge, and the suffering people experience in trying to live according to these values, as well as how to meet their particular needs with loving compassion."

Theologian Christine Hinze, who engages in such work, sounds an important note of caution in this endeavor. She says, "Undertaking bridge discourse is risky; one takes the chance of offending, or being written off, by everyone. No matter how sincerely attempted, building bridges or hybrid publics across ideological differences is arduous and uncertain work. But amid our fractious cultures, we are deeply interconnected, and grave issues urgently require our collaborative attention."[6] It is my hope that more of us will join others who are already lifting up American Catholics' growing diversity, together with a renewed sense of unity, in this church that James Joyce once described as "Here comes everybody."

---

[6] Christine Firer Hinze, *Glass Ceilings and Dirt Floors: Women, Work, and the Global Economy* (New York: Paulist Press, 2015), 24.

Part 1

This Moment in the Church

1
Reflections on This Moment in the Church

The reflections gathered in this chapter are responses to our request for prominent Catholic thinkers to share their perspectives on divisions that exist in the US Catholic Church today. Their brief essays were originally delivered as opening remarks to the 2015 Polarization in the US Catholic Church conference at the University of Notre Dame.

We asked contributors to respond to the following questions: How do you see the US church today, at this moment in time? From your experience, why might it be important for people with differing views to talk with one another about polarization in the church—and how might we do that? What are your hopes for what such conversations might accomplish? What situations or issues deserve special attention? What strategies might lead us, as a church, beyond polarization?

Each contributor speaks from his or her particular experiences and concerns. Together, they offer a portrait of the problems and promise of the US Catholic Church today.

Reflection by Most Reverend Daniel Flores

There is perhaps too much gravity and not enough levity in our circles these days. I would go so far as to suggest at the outset that until we have reached a point wherein we can actually laugh together and enjoy the simple and primary gift of being together in the same world, the same church, and the same room, then it is not yet time to discuss the issues that divide. Therefore, I want to take a path through a few key words and phrases and see where that leads.

"Polarization" is an interesting term. We are using it as a stand-in term for something that we perceive as a perduring presence in contemporary church life in the United States. The editors of this volume have described a phenomenon of divisiveness and vitriol in our local churches and in the national discourse within the church.

We are borrowing the term "polarization" from the language of political science, which has adopted it to speak of a tendency for extremes of opposition to at times dominate a political discourse. But political and social sciences appear to have adopted the paradigm from the field of the physical sciences, where the term implies a separation to opposing fields, occurring by a kind of natural repulsion. The term is also used in optic science, as when describing the behavior of light or sound waves. It is worth noting that both magnetic polar behavior and wave patterns are natural and, in this universe anyway, inevitable phenomena.

I suspect that in the social and political sciences, some would argue that the coalescing of extremes is an inevitable manifestation in the generation and degeneration of social dynamics. Perhaps we can examine critically if shadows of inevitable social dynamics color our optics on how we look at church life.

Thus it seems that we want to talk openly about our experience of the church as excessively marked by division into something like polar opposites. Maybe polarization is the best term, or maybe there is a better way to talk about it. I do not know.

As a way of beginning the conversation, though, I should like to invite us to revisit how the Christian theological tradition has attempted to grapple with what we are trying to name and help heal. Thomas Aquinas would probably identify it with the term *discordia*. Now discord, theologically speaking, cannot be understood in isolation from the Christian virtue it opposes: namely, *concordia*. Concord is an effect of charity that leads to the union of wills. Discord is a disruption of that union of wills. Thomas notes pointedly, however, that concord is the union of wills infused with charity, not necessarily the union of opinions: *Concordia quae est caritatis effectus est unio voluntatum, non unio opinionum.*[1] As far as Thomas is concerned, difference of opinions need not disrupt the union of wills. Related to *discordia*, the contradiction of wills, is the problem of contentiousness, which is the contradictive use of words: saying things that are by design opposed to the charitable union of wills.[2] And then there is *rixa*, actions designed to undermine the union of charity. This seems to be the extreme in the vices opposed to concord, because it is like an enduring private war.[3]

Now then, I would add into the mix the fact that familial language was adopted early in the Christian community. Identifying one another as brothers, sisters, fathers, and mothers is profoundly interwoven into the New Testament record. Late Pauline writings speak of the household of the faith. Without entering into a cultural exegesis about what such terms implied in first-century Jewish, Greek, Roman milieu, it seems safe to say that Christians wanted to convey a series of relationships that were stable and had God as author. In Scripture, familial language is complemented, and perhaps corrected, by the language of friendship and the vocabulary of charity: see how they love one another. Taken together, the language of Scripture suggests that we are connected by relationships rooted in a prior bond willed and forged by Christ. Baptism links the members to Christ and, through him, to all the other members

[1] Thomas Aquinas, *Summa Theologiae*, II–II, q. 37, a. 1, ad. c.
[2] Ibid., II–II, q. 38.
[3] Ibid., II–II, q. 41.

of the community of believers. These bonds are further characterized by a kind of friendship marked by the New Testament
charity of mutual yielding. Charity is the virtue that gives life
to the relation willed by Christ. Without it, we are living a
show, and the world rightly dismisses us as no different from
any other show on television.

I would place on the table my sense that the wounds that
divide us are rooted in the loss of confidence that the members
of the household of the faith actually love one another. And I
think that this loss of confidence is particularly striking when
we are talking about relations that imply authority of some
kind. In short, we are living in the midst of an ecclesial loss of
confidence that fathers in the church love their children and
that children love their fathers.

Thus, I think I would name the wound as one that especially strikes at our relation to the father, particularly as the
one who is in some way responsible for the governing of the
household. If both sons in the parable of the prodigal son had
faith in the love of the father, then both would have been at
the party. As it happens, only one had that faith; the other is
left thinking it over. Hence, the doubt about the love of the
father is reflected also in a doubt about whether the children
actually love each other. In the parable, there are evidently
signs of discord between the brothers; and in the case of the
older brother, this is based on a prior discord in his relation to
the father. Doubtless, the parable is primarily aimed at forming
our perceptions of the merciful God who is Father. Yet if the
parable cannot in some way find an analogous application to
the mystery of relationality of the church, we are thinking, I
think, too univocally.

If the first thing you believe about your father is that he
loves you, then the adult conversations you have with him are
likely to be of a tone and content not overly marked by easy
categorization and facile dismissals. This is true whether we
are talking about our natural father or our bishop. If the first
thing a father believes about his adult children is that they

love him and are disposed to be patient with him, then the conversations are less likely to be defensive and rancorous.

That our current struggles with discord and contentious-ness, not to mention *rixa*, coincide with a wider cultural breakdown in familial cohesiveness is, at least, worth noting. What might be helpful is to begin identifying how cultural categories that are not necessarily compatible with the Gospel have corroded our sense of the primacy of charity and mercy within the household of the church. Right, left, conservative, traditionalist, radical, intransigent, liberal, etc., are all exam-ples of descriptive terms that exempt the person from the trial of actually having to listen to and know the other person, as person, and as person related to me. We should note and then lament the loss of a discourse of respect and affection. All of this leads me to propose that the uncritical adoption of politi-cal paradigms for our discourse tragically serves to preempt the Gospel primacy of relation.

For us, the first question is not "what are you?" It is, rather, "who are you to me?" And for the Christian, the answer is al-ways the same; you are my brother, and you are my sister. You are my father, and you are my child. You are my mother, and I am your son or daughter. The relation is prior "in being" to the conversation and to the disagreement. But if the relation is not apprehended at the start of the discussion, what happens then? We might as well ask what happens when salt goes flat.

The Christian primacy of relation should be understood in the context of the wider aim of the New Law, which is the grace of the Holy Spirit. Its aim has always been the infusion of new life into old and wounded relations: relations with God, a Trinity of Persons, and with one another. The praxis of mercy, so central to Pope Francis's preaching and life, begins at home. The relation is prior, but for us, it is not so easily acknowl-edged. The father has to ask if he is governing with the mercy of the kingdom and accept the fact that his adult children may rightly ask him that question. The son or daughter outside the party also has to ask for a grace to see things differently: that, in the end, a father who loves can make many mistakes, but he will not cease being my father, in the full affectionate use of the term. Without a renewal in the primacy of relation in our dealings with one another, the church fades into the grey pragmatism of ordinary life, indistinguishable from a world convinced that social dynamics and human relations are governed by some social law unaffected by the redemption.

Reflection by Reverend John I. Jenkins, CSC

As a university president, I get letters. Many of them complain about everything from the cost of higher education to the win-loss record of our football team. But I'm struck by the fact that often the most personal and vitriolic letters come from fellow devout Catholics.

Of course, committed Catholics are more likely to be the ones who care most about what the priest-president of a major Catholic university does or does not do. And I accept that many of my decisions merit scrutiny and criticism. So I understand why they write. But why is the language so harsh . . . so personal? Why does the most caustic language come from sisters and brothers with whom I share a faith in Christ and am called, in the church, to build a civilization of love?

Now Catholics certainly do not have a monopoly on polarizing rhetoric, and I think our divisions are best understood in the context of wider polarization in society that leads to much of the nastiness in the public forum and political dysfunction. What is it at work here? Harsh, polarizing rhetoric in the political sphere is not formulated to convince those who are the target of the attacks. No clear-thinking politician thinks he is going to win over opponents by calling them depraved and misguided. The language is intended, rather, to galvanize the like-minded in a common antipathy. Why? A political tactician knows that she needs only 50 percent plus one vote of those who go to the polls to actually vote. There is no point to gaining favor with those on the other end of the political spectrum. Moreover, she or he needs to sufficiently motivate supporters to give money, to campaign, and to go vote. The polarizing language identifies a threat that must be defeated; it aims to motivate the like-minded to bond together in vanquishing the threat.

Catholic America often mimics, I think, the practices of our political life. And it stands out in the degree to which it possesses one important resource to make the rhetoric effective. Vilification of opponents requires a rich, common moral framework. It demands the language of ultimacy. I can only convince you that someone else is evil if you and I agree on what is good and evil and that what is at stake is of great significance. The issue may be abortion, the plight of the poor, the nature of marriage, or the centrality of the family. In these and other cases, religion generally, and Catholicism in particular, gives a rich, moral framework to motivate the like-minded and to portray opponents as misguided people, threatening all we hold most dear.

I would add that these tendencies become particularly virulent, I think, when a religious agenda becomes adjoined to a political agenda. The United States is a religious country, and political leaders have always used religious language to describe our national aspirations. Politicians have a great interest in marshaling religious groups for their purposes, and religious leaders, understandably, want to exert influence through ascending political leaders and their movements. Politicians, however, naturally think in election cycles and may not worry much about the collateral damage of losing political campaigns as long as they win.

Religious leaders, on the other hand, should think in terms of the cycle of salvation history and be concerned with building a church that witnesses to Christ as we wait for his return. I believe that when the church has aligned itself throughout history, when it has aligned itself too closely with political leaders, movements, and regimes of the left or the right, it has usually been the church that has suffered in the long run. We must, of course, be engaged in the world and its issues, and that means being engaged in political discussions. But I recommend that we all periodically engage in an examination of conscience regarding our rhetoric and whether it serves, truly, the unity we have in Christ, who is the only King.

Now, a political realist may respond to these reflections and say, "Look, politics in a democratic society is a full-contact sport. Not a game for wimps." And the history of Christianity is certainly full of violent conflicts, even of killing one another, as Christians in previous generations did. So, the realist tells us, "Stop your hand-wringing and save your pious platitudes. Man up," as our students say, "and jump into the fray and the joy of mudslinging."

What are we to say to that? I find an analysis of Robert Putnam and a colleague of ours, David Campbell, here at Notre Dame, in their book *American Grace*, persuasive.[4] According to them, the social revolution of the 1960s brought two aftershocks. The first was the conservatism of the 1980s, led by Ronald Reagan, which set up the culture war conflicts. The second, however, was the movement, particularly among young people, away from established religion and the growth of the "nones," those who, when asked about religious affiliation, say they have none. Fed up with conflicts surrounding religion and its values, it seems, these young people are checking out of organized religion, leading to the weakening of our churches.

The church is viewed among many, as in the words of my friend and colleague, John Cavadini, as something less than the sum of its controversies. Seen that way, who needs it? So while polarizing rhetoric is used effectively by people to serve their interests, I believe it's poisonous for the church. I think Pope Francis is right when he says that people come to the church through attraction. But the acrimony of many of our

---

[4] Robert D. Putnam and David E. Campbell, *American Grace: How Religion Divides and Unites Us* (New York: Simon and Schuster, 2010).

conversations obscures the beauty of the church; it attracts few and drives away many. We must act to serve our true interest, which is the true salvation of our souls and the coming of the reign of God.

Reflection by Julie Hanlon Rubio

Those of us who want to see more unity in the church hope that we can get "beyond polarization." One key assumption for us is that people perceive more division than there actually is, in part because they focus on so-called "hot button" issues. This is important, because if we are closer together than we realize, constructive dialogue is more possible than it sounds. To some extent, I share this presumption. For most of my career, I have avoided "hot button" issues in my field of family ethics. I have found that when it comes to dilemmas of ordinary life, most Catholics have shared hopes and worries. There is plenty we can talk about.

Still, I don't think it is possible to ignore "hot button" issues. For we also presume that in order to heal, we have to name the wounds that push us apart. Issues related to sex and gender are sources of wounds for many Catholics. We have to talk about them before we can move toward common ground in the church.

What do we mean by "church"? Do we include those who do not attend Mass regularly, as well as those who have in some way distanced themselves from the church, those to whom some researchers give the labels "disaffiliating" or "de-converting"?[5] Many of these people still have some relationship to Catholicism. My inclination is not to exclude them when we talk about polarization in the church.

---

[5] Patrick Hornbeck, Tom Beaudoin, and William Portier, "Deconversion and Disaffiliation in Contemporary US Roman Catholicism," *Horizons* 40, no. 2 (December 2013): 255–92. Beaudoin defines deconversion as "[T]he process by which baptized Catholics change their ways of affiliating with the Church or the faith." Ibid., 256.

If we talk to those on the edges, we will hear a lot about sex and gender. The sexual abuse scandal is, by many accounts, their most pressing concern.[6] Many are alienated by Catholic positions on issues of sexual ethics. Some are very uncomfortable being associated with an institution that has an all-male leadership team.[7] Even if people do not always cite these issues as primary reasons for their distance from the church, when they criticize the church for "hypocrisy" and "focus[ing] too much on rules," they are probably not thinking of Catholic Social Teaching.[8] Wounds relating to sex and gender lead many to walk away, even if not to completely shut the door.[9]

But even if we go to the most committed, we will still find concern about sex and gender. Polarization can be most

[6] Pew Research Center, "U.S. Catholics See Sex Abuse as the Church's Most Important Problem, Charity as Its Most Important Contribution," *Pew Forum*, March 6, 2013, http://www.pewforum.org/2013/03/06/us-catholics -see-sex-abuse-as-the-churchs-most-important-problem-charity-as-its-most -important-contribution/.

[7] See Patricia Wittberg, "A Lost Generation?," *America* magazine 206, no. 5 (February 20, 2012), http://americamagazine.org/issue/5129/article /lost-generation, for one sociologist's account of why Millennial women are practicing less than their male counterparts even though they are more spiritual. See Helen Alvare, *Breaking Through: Catholic Women Speak for Themselves* (Huntington, IN: Our Sunday Visitor, 2012) for an account of the joys and difficulties experienced by more traditional Catholic women. For more progressive voices, see Kate Dugan and Jennifer Owens, *From the Pews in the Back: Young Women and Catholicism* (Collegeville, MN: Liturgical Press, 2009); Angela Bonavoglia, *Good Catholic Girls: How Women Are Leading the Fight to Change the Church* (New York: HarperOne, 2006).

[8] See Beaudoin, Hornbeck, and Portier, "Deconversion and Disaffiliation," and Pew Research Center, "'Nones' on the Rise," *Pew Forum*, October 9, 2012, http://www.pewforum.org/2012/10/09/nones-on-the-rise/. Around 60 percent of the unaffiliated do not attend services because of disagreements with the church, "hypocrisy," or overly demanding leaders who "focus too much on rules." In all likelihood, sex is the key area for disagreement.

[9] Pew Research Center, "Changing Attitudes on Gay Marriage," *Pew Forum*, September 24, 2014, http://www.pewforum.org/2014/09/24/graphics -slideshow-changing-attitudes-on-gay-marriage/.

pronounced among those who are most deeply invested. In a recent book comparing two representative Catholic parishes, one traditionally conservative, the other self-consciously progressive, sociologist Mary Ellen Konieczny found that views and practices related to sex, marriage, and child-rearing were crucial to the religious self-understanding of both groups and to their alienation from those on the other side.[10]

At the same time, polarization may look different for African American and Latino Catholics. In many of their communities, concerns about inequality, immigration, hyperincarceration, and racism trump or reshape concerns about sex and gender. These issues are often not prioritized by white, middle-class Catholics who champion or question family values, yet they affect people's ability to form and sustain strong families.

This is precisely why the Synod on the Family was so important. Pope Francis understood that it was in relation to family that people most needed the church to be merciful. The synod was significant because of its process. In preparation for it, Catholics throughout the world were given the opportunity to answer survey questions asking them if they understood and accepted Catholic teaching. Many were happy to see the church open itself to conversation and encourage vigorous debate among the bishops.[11]

Yet the synod also suggests the difficulty of moving beyond controversial issues. Attempts to soften the language used to talk about gay and lesbian Catholics, as well as proposals to allow some divorced and remarried Catholics to return to the sacraments, were greeted with jubilation by some and great consternation by others. One commentator wrote that if these proposals were accepted, it would "put the Church on the brink

[10] Mary Ellen Konieczny, *The Spirit's Tether: Family, Work and Religion among American Catholics* (Oxford: Oxford University Press, 2013).

[11] See Julie H. Rubio, "U.S. Catholic Hopes for the Upcoming Synod on the Family," INTAMS Review 20, no. 1 (2014): 13–18.

of a precipice," encouraging doubt and confusion.[12] Meanwhile, others worried that the synod would conclude without changing anything.[13] Controversy divided us once again.

While it is tempting to look the other way, we can't dismiss sex and gender issues. We have to listen: to those deeply wounded by sexual abuse; to young adults alienated by church teachings on premarital sex and cohabitation; to married couples who see contraception as consistent with their strong commitment to self-giving love and fruitfulness; to single parents struggling against the odds; to all who long for a church with women leaders; to gay, lesbian, and transgender Catholics who experience the pain of exclusion.

Yet we also have to listen to those who stand with the church and against the culture on these very same issues and, increasingly, feel unable to speak lest they be labeled intolerant. It is in relation to sex, marriage, and gender that people feel judged, excluded, and alienated, no matter which side they are on.

Of course, we cannot stay here, not if staying means debating rules. Instead, we have to bracket some debates and move to a space where progress is possible.

On sexuality, can we talk about just and loving relationships? Can we follow Pope Francis and "care for the grain" without "grow[ing] impatient at the weeds"?[14] Can we talk

---

[12] Ross Douthat, "The Pope and the Precipice," *New York Times*, October 25, 2014, http://www.nytimes.com/2014/10/26/opinion/sunday/ross-douthat-the-pope-and-the-precipice.html?_r=0. See also Jeanne Smits, "Exclusive Interview: Cardinal Burke Says Confusion Spreading among Catholics 'in an Alarming Way'," *LifeSiteNews*, March 24, 2015, https://www.lifesitenews.com/news/exclusive-interview-cardinal-burke-says-confusion-spreading-among-catholics.

[13] Elisabetta Povoledo, "Women See Themselves as Left Out amid Talk of Change in the Catholic Church," *New York Times*, March 6, 2015, http://www.nytimes.com/2015/03/07/world/women-see-themselves-as-left-out-amid-talk-of-change-in-catholic-church.html?_r=0.

[14] Francis, Apostolic Exhortation *Evangelii Gaudium* (On the Proclamation of the Gospel in Today's World), November 24, 2013, http://w2.vatican.va

about how to help people increase their capacities to express love and practice fidelity, in and outside of marriage? Can we talk about the social structures that are needed to support families living in poverty?

On gender, can we focus on discipleship? Can we talk about how women and men can best utilize their gifts in their families and society? Can we work together to reduce sexual violence and abortion, to find space for women leaders in the church?

I do not mean to suggest that this sort of bracketing is easy or without controversy. But is it possible? If it is possible, if we manage to make any progress during this moment and beyond, it will be because we embrace Pope Francis's profound understanding of church. Near the end of *Evangelii Gaudium*, the pope exhorts us to cultivate "a willingness to face conflict head on," "to build communion amid disagreement," and "to see others in their deepest dignity."[15] This is what we saw him encourage at the synod.

In his final speech, after claiming, remarkably, that it would have been "disappointing not to have debate like this," he said,

> This is the Church . . . who is not afraid to roll up her sleeves to pour oil and wine on people's wounds; who doesn't see humanity as a house of glass to judge or categorize people. . . . It is the Church that is not afraid to eat and drink with prostitutes and [tax collectors]. The Church that has the doors wide open to receive the needy, the penitent, and not only the just or those who believe they are perfect![16]

/content/francesco/en/apost_exhortations/documents/papa-francesco
_esortazione-ap_20131124_evangelii-gaudium.html, 24.

[15] Ibid., 9, 10.

[16] Francis, "Address of His Holiness Pope Francis for the Conclusion of the Third Extraordinary General Assembly of the Synod of Bishops," October 18, 2014, https://w2.vatican.va/content/francesco/en/speeches/2014/october/documents/papa-francesco_20141018_conclusione-sinodo-dei-vescovi.html.

This is the church. This is the vision we have to keep in front of us. It will give us courage to name the wounds as we know them and seek healing not in walking away but in striving for unity.

Reflection by Christian Smith

My perspective—and the point I want to make in this larger conversation—is very specific. I do not speak as a theologian or a pastoral leader but as a sociologist. We in social science have the idea of the need to always do first what we call "establish the phenomenon." That means that, before explaining and responding to something, it is necessary to take the time to really figure out *what* exactly the something *is* that we think we are explaining and responding to. There is no use explaining something that is not true or is different than what we think we are explaining. Helping in one specific way to more precisely "establish the phenomenon" of polarization in the Catholic Church for this constructive conversation is the one contribution that I want to make here.

My view can be summarized by saying that the polarization we are discussing is not evenly distributed across age cohorts of Catholics. Different generations of Catholics can and often do have different issues that concern them. So it is important that Catholics of certain age cohorts not project onto those of other ages "their issues," assuming that everyone else cares as much about their issues as they do. Here, I am using the language of generations. A group of good Catholic sociologists have studied American Catholicism long before I came along, people like William D'Antonio and James D. Davidson, who have made the idea of *generations* central to their analyses. I commend their work because I think generation is an important lens through which to understand issues like polarization.

Here is my main point: the kind of polarization we are talking about in this conversation, I think, often revolves around certain issues that were salient in the Vatican II era and its aftermath. For a certain generation, especially Baby Boomers, Vatican II opened up new possibilities and raised hopes and expectations, and for some, those were disappointed. Many Catholics of that era responded by veering leftward and rightward and have been in disagreement and conflict ever since. The next generation, typically called Generation X, followed by heading in many directions, too. Some simply dropped out of the church entirely, on the one hand, and others, inspired by Pope John Paul II, became even more conservative than their parents.

But the generation I wish to focus on here is even younger: those we call Millennials, or youth who are now in their twenties and early thirties. For the most part, compared to earlier, Vatican II–oriented generations, the vast majority of Millennial Catholics simply do not care that much about the Roman Catholic Church as an institution, its official policies and politics. They are not generally hostile to the church, not antagonistic or fundamentally dissenting. It is more a matter of general indifference. Conflict in polarization requires expending resources for some issue about which one really cares. Most Millennials simply do not care or know enough about the church to engage in that kind of conflict.

For many Catholic Millennials, even committed Catholics, one common background assumption they make that neutralizes their taking sides in polarized debates is that any religious faith is very personal, even individual or private—not something institutional or shared. They are aware, of course, that religions are institutionalized, but as far as the vast majority of young Catholics today are concerned, the institution of church is sort of like its packaging. What really matters is what is "inside," which may seem most authentic. The packaging can end up in the recycling bin, for all they care. And so they are not so invested in some of the issues and politics over which other Catholics are contentiously polarized. Many perceive that these are institutional, bureaucratic matters; and, as far as they think, their religious faith and practice is an individual, personal matter that does not have to engage larger collective policies and practices of the church.

Millennials are also generally sick of culture wars. Anything that smacks of culture warring simply does not interest them. If something feels culture wars-y, for the most part, they turn off. Most are tired of conflict and just wish everyone could get along. Part of this, I think, stems from a legitimate weariness of interminable adult fighting. Another part of it grows out of strong forms of relativism about knowledge and morality, which they have deeply imbibed. Most Millennials believe that each person can decide for themselves what they think, which is fine, but that nobody has the right to be judgmental in criticizing what anyone else thinks. Most views that people might hold are thought to be legitimate "for them." And if differences of views among people create problems, then everyone should just back away, keep their beliefs quietly to themselves, and just get along pragmatically.

Related to the issue of their individualistic approach to faith, many young Catholics are very localist in the way they understand life, not really tuned into issues in the Catholic Church broadly. For example, we first interviewed teenagers right around the time that the priest abuse scandal was all over the news. We were expecting to hear a lot of blowback and anger from them about it but, to our surprise, the vast majority of Catholic teenagers were not disturbed. They often said something like, "Yeah, there are always some bad people in any institution, but it's not a big deal. My priest is a great guy; I like and trust the people I know." That was the standard attitude. When people live in such very local worlds, there is less on their horizon about which to become polarized.

Furthermore, more than a few American Catholics of the Millennial generation literally do not understand much about the content of polarizing issues, because they were never educated much in specific church teachings. I know that, given the stereotypes, this may sound amazing, but I have interviewed young American Catholics who with straight faces reported to me that as far as they knew, the Catholic Church has no particular teaching on sexual issues. They do not dissent against church teachings because they have not been educated well enough to know even what they might or might not dissent against.

Of course, to balance this view, we must also recognize that there exists a serious, committed minority of Catholic Millennials who are very invested in the church and its policies and politics. We might think of them as "JPII-type" of youth, following behind their counterparts in the Generation X age cohort, and many of them *are* polarized, most often on the right. But statistically, they are quite rare. As a proportion of the whole, they are very small. To some Catholic leaders, they may appear more numerous, because such youth tend to gravitate to places where the leaders live and work and to be drawn to certain kinds of older Catholics with whom they identify. But, in that case, this means that those older Catholics likely have what we in social science call a "bad sampling bias." That is, they think the world is a certain way based on their limited sample, but that view is biased because of the particular kind of people that tend to surround them. So, while there does exist an important minority of younger Catholics who would fit the polarization model, we should not lose sight of the fact that they are a small minority. For the vast majority of Millennial Catholics, the question is not fighting for issues they believe in within a church framework but general indifference and disconnection.

Consider this one statistic from a report I recently helped to produce along with the University of Notre Dame Institute for Church Life. I conducted a study over ten years of a nationally representative sample of teenagers, the National Study of Youth and Religion (NSYR), which we followed as they grew up into their twenties. Of all those who identified as Catholic as teenagers, ten years later, one-half of them no longer identified as Catholic. That is a 50 percent attrition rate for young Catholics. That loss speaks volumes about how invested Catholic youth are in their church. Many—if not most—young people being raised as Catholics today have concerns, orientations, and assumptions that are disconnected from many of the things that older generations of Catholics care about. The challenge is not whether polarization among them can be reduced, but whether they know and care enough about anything related to the church to invest in taking any stand on any of it.

To summarize, the kind of issue-polarization among US Catholics that has concerned many within the church is not evenly distributed across age cohorts of Americans. I suggest that it is most intense among American Catholics of the Vatican II generation and probably some of their children, as well as a minority of Generation Xers. Findings from my research suggest that, by contrast, Catholic youth today, with some exceptions, do not seem particularly caught up mentally or emotionally in issues that often polarize older Catholics. This is explained by a set of related facts. First, relatively few young US Catholics are invested enough in their faith and church to care very much about issues that divide Catholics. It simply does not mean enough to most of them to get worked up about such issues. Second, most Catholic teenagers and emerging adults already know what they personally believe about contentious issues and—operating something like "opinion libertarians"—feel no need to struggle to convince others to share their views. Very few assume that the church has binding teaching authority to shape conscience, so they are comfortable with a "live and let live" attitude. Third, many Catholic youth are so poorly catechized or otherwise informed that they may not know exactly what the Catholic Church teaches on specific issues and what the reasonable possible alternatives are. Fourth, more generally, most American youth, especially Catholic youth, have absorbed a normative belief in a version of tolerance that makes them reluctant to get into arguments or "judge" anyone else.

Catholicism for most American Catholic youth is thus one identity and set of practices among many others that they may or may not care very much about or wish to invest in. The few exceptions to the above generalization are those teenagers raised by parents who are very invested in Catholic culture, and often culture wars issues, and who identify with their parents' views closely enough to care to make issues of them. But those Catholic youth are relatively very few.

In short, Catholic polarization presupposes minimum levels of investment, commitment, and knowledge for such polarizing conflicts to make sense and be worth fighting over, conditions which seem to have pertained among some Baby Boomer Catholics, some of their children, and some in Generation X, but generally do not among Millennials today.

Reflection by Michael Sean Winters

French Catholic philosopher Jacques Maritain once said that we are born into the world with a liberal heart or a conservative heart; it is not something we can change. But he also suggested that we spend considerable time acquainting ourselves with the kind of heart with which we were not born, to study and sympathize with the concerns that grow from that other kind of heart, in our search for wisdom.

I think that it is incumbent on us, as Catholics, to follow Maritain's advice insofar as we wish to acquire wisdom. I also think that this exercise helps build up the unity of the church. None of us has a monopoly on wisdom, and all of us benefit from forging friendships with those who are different from us. The more we recognize this, the more likely a difference of opinion will not eat at the unity of the church. But that effort does not obliterate the fact that good Catholics do have different kinds of fundamental dispositions.

Sometimes these dispositions are rooted not in our birth but in our circumstances. In his new book, *The Archaeology of Faith*, Fr. Lou Cameli writes about his grandparents who were sharecroppers in Italy. He writes:

Take for example, the conservative mind-set that quite naturally belongs to farmers. Time and work on the farm are keyed to a steady rhythm of the seasons with planting, growing, harvesting, and letting the land lie fallow—until the cycle begins again. Even individual days have their fixed set of routines from sunrise to sunset. Fixed cycles and predictable patterns enable farmers to live from the land. When the unexpected breaks in, disrupting a set routine—such as accidents that disable workers or bad weather that halts the growth of crops—farmers feel a deep sense of devastation, perhaps accompanied by anger or hopelessness.[17]

Farmers are naturally conservative, but most of us are no longer farmers. And, when I read his comment about bad weather producing anger or hopelessness, I thought of Cardinal Kasper speaking at Catholic University last autumn, when he said many churchmen look at the current papacy as a bit of bad weather, and they are just waiting for it to pass. My point is that insofar as the church is a human institution, it is not helpful to paper over differences that are real. The current practice at *America* magazine of forbidding writers to use the terms "liberal" or "conservative" seems foolish to me. Adjectives, like all metaphors, can either enlighten or obscure. But I do not see how the cause of unity is furthered by making poor James Martin, SJ, write, "some writers, like George Weigel and Robbie George," rather than just writing, "some conservative writers." Adjectives can be misused, but that does not mean they are useless, only that they should be used with care. So let's not forget that human beings tend to incline toward a more conservative sense of the world or a more liberal sense of the world, and the church must be comfortable with, walk with, and learn from both kinds of people.

My second point follows from the first. I want to push back a bit against the idea that polarization today is such a

---

[17] Louis J. Cameli, *The Archaeology of Faith: A Personal Exploration of How We Come to Believe* (Notre Dame, IN: Ave Maria Press 2015), 35.

huge problem. As much as we moderns flatter ourselves that our problems are singularly more difficult than those faced by previous generations of Catholics, on this issue, the case cannot be made.

In the last years of the nineteenth century and first years of the twentieth, a woman named Ella Edes worked in Rome at the *Propaganda Fide*, which then was in charge of episcopal appointments in the United States. Thankfully, her correspondence was largely preserved, and I rely here on Gerald Fogarty's history of relations between the Holy See and the American hierarchy to tell the tale.[18] When the rector of the North American College, Monsignor—later Cardinal—William Henry O'Connell was conniving to have himself appointed the bishop of Portland, Maine, Edes wrote to Michael Corrigan, the archbishop of New York. "Monsignor Pomposity is so invariably rude, ill-bred, and disobliging . . . I do not suppose he knows any better, being low-born and common, pitch-forked, suddenly, to a position which has turned his head. Like all under-bred Paddies, I am not, in his eyes, sufficiently rich, or fashionable to be treated with even ordinary courtesy."

Her judgment of the rising cleric did not soften with time, and when, in 1906, O'Connell got himself named coadjutor to Archbishop Williams in Boston, she wrote to Bishop McQuaid of Rochester, "I have no doubt that Pomposity paid well, Falconio, Merry del Val, and especially, Satolli, and that they seized the moment when Cardinal Gotti is lying at the point of death to carry out their designs." She urged the bishops of the Boston Province to "resolutely show their teeth, and not suffer their noble Metropolitan to be thus grossly insulted & shamefully treated, simply to promote the selfish aims and inordinate ambition, and gratify the shameless cupidity of Italian cardinal & Roman officials!" She proposed a remedy, telling McQuaid of an Irish bishop who brought to mind the

---

[18] Gerald P. Fogarty, *The Vatican and the American Hierarchy from 1870 to 1965* (Collegeville, MN: Liturgical Press, 1985).

names of recalcitrant priests at Mass and mentally placed them in the chalice, leaving them to God's disposition. "And they die off like flies!" Journalists today would be fired even if they tweeted such sentiments.

I do not suggest that we all imitate the special viciousness of Ms. Edes in her letters. But her forcefully stated views were not idiosyncratic. Divisions within the church in the United States at the turn of the last century were real, and the fights were fierce, with the Americanizers like Gibbons, Ireland, and Keane on one side and the conservatives like Corrigan allied with German Catholics on the other. They fought about everything. Cardinal O'Connell really did try and have Rome squash the nascent bishops' conference. Ms. Edes was deeply personal in her invective, though it should be noted she was often right. Cardinal O'Connell really was pompous.

There are times, I admit, when I feel a similar desire to lash out at another person. But it is best to confine the lashing out to differing ideas and arguments and not to the person. Sometimes people, especially commentators, receive an attack on their argument as an ad hominem attack because our arguments are so close to our personalities that we have difficulty distinguishing. The old yarn about "hating the sin but loving the sinner" always was, and still is, cold comfort. But some of my regular disputants deploy the "hate the sin, love the sinner" line against those whose sexual behavior does not match the Christian ideal, and surely sexuality is as close to a person's personality as their arguments are. Here is my rule of thumb: Try to keep the focus on the arguments, but if you decide the situation deserves a sharp elbow, remember the sage advice that if you are going to sin, sin boldly. To get under an ideologue's skin, make sure you mock. It drives them nuts.

My third point has to do with the special role of the Catholic commentariat: people like myself who police the culture and traffic in opinions. I do not think we should shy away from good, passionate debate. Dull prose is as much of a literary sin as throwing a sharp elbow is a sin against church unity. It is the shape of the debate that matters. Our public discourse benefits not only from debate but also from debate that seeks deeper understanding and, hopefully, eventually, even fleetingly, consensus. I like to say that while people at the extremes are certainly capable of making important and interesting arguments, they also are usually incapable of driving the discussion in fruitful or practical ways. It is at the center of American church life that the important conversations have to happen—and there has been very little room in the center. One of the important failings of the American hierarchy has been their willingness to coddle the extremes on the right, such as LifeSiteNews, or the Becket Fund, or EWTN. The "center" is pretty far to the right at the moment. But the winds have changed, and some of us view the current pontificate not as bad weather but as a time of sunny skies. It is my hope that the leaders of the church will use this change of weather to create the space and the climate for a discussion in the center. Pope Francis is encouraging debate and discussion. I commend the editors of this volume for attempting to do precisely that.

I would submit that there should a price of admission to that conversation. Actually, two prices. First, participants must be Catholics first, people who do not distort the church's teachings to serve an extraneous ideological or political agenda. They must operate intellectually from what Fr. Robert Imbelli calls the "Christic imagination" and have their arguments rooted in our Catholic intellectual tradition. Second, participants must be willing to call out their own side, their own team, and to do so with some regularity. We journalists hold forth the ideal without fear or favor, and this should apply especially to members of the Catholic commentariat when the teachings of the church challenge those with whom we tend to agree on any political or social issues. Once those two prices of admission are paid, I think a fruitful dialogue can take place.

So, two cheers for attempts to constrain polarization within the church. But, I also have to say: When George Weigel calls that beautiful Mass at the border last year—with those powerful images of Cardinal Sean O'Malley and Bishop Jerry Kicanas distributing Holy Communion through the slats of the border fence—when Mr. Weigel calls that Mass "an act of political theater," I am going to call him out on it, and if that increases the degree of perceived polarization, so be it. As long as we walk through this vale of tears, sometimes our values are incommensurate. Thank you, Isaiah Berlin. We know that we seek, but will never attain, the unity of all knowledge. And in the meantime, sometimes we need to have strong, even polarizing, debates about the state of our church and the issues that should concern us as followers of the Master.

Let me end on a more cheerful note. A couple years back, I had to write a review of a book that I found not very good. The author, whom I did not know, replied. I replied. Polarization in spades. Then, last December, the Holy Father gave a talk in which he called all of us to reach out to those in the church from whom we were alienated. Through the good offices of a mutual friend, I reached out to this author and suggested we grab a cup of coffee together. We had a thoroughly enjoyable two hours of engaged, nonconfrontational conversation and pledged to do it again. I look around the room here and see people whom I met originally because of a disagreement about something they or I had written. They have become not only good friends but also people to whom I turn when I wish to deepen my understanding of a contentious issue. I always learn something from my encounters. They help me follow the counsel of Maritain I cited at the beginning. I am a better writer and a better Catholic for these friendships. But, I think the fact that we first met on the occasion of an instance of polarization shows that it is possible to move forward, not into any homogenized Catholic identity or shared intellectual agreement, but into our respective Catholic identities, more intelligently as well as more kindly, by engaging. We should fear the isolation and separation of different groups within the church as much as we fear the inevitable polarizing conflicts that come with engagement. And, at the end of the day, we will all throw ourselves on the mercy of God.

2

The Scars to Prove It

Michael McGillicuddy

I am not an academic, not a journalist, not a church worker. My perspective is influenced by three identities: I am a social worker, I am a culture war veteran, and I am "between."

As a social worker, I know that hurt people hurt people, but I also know that hurt people can heal. I see what happens when people who feel safe and share a common bond spend time together in deep conversation. Social work practice emphasizes the critical importance of cultural competence, of deeply understanding other cultures on their own terms. It is extremely challenging to "get" those worldviews that most diverge from our own, yet we must summon the curiosity and humility to do so. Moreover, social work is grounded in behavioral science research confirming that our emotions have an outsized influence on our reasoning. Jon Haidt's work on intuitionist moral reasoning is compelling in this regard, and social psychology has broad applications to the task at hand today.

The culture war trope is overdone. Think about it: the insistence that one's adversaries are "culture warriors" has itself become a formidable weapon in the culture war! And yet, the phrase persists. It is deeply woven into our conversations about polarization, and I think that we are stuck with it for now. But if we're going to speak of culture war, we must also speak of its collateral damage. I am a casualty of two Catholic culture war skirmishes—one in the '60s, the other in the '80s—and I have the scars to prove it. These scars have dogged me over the years. I have never shed the resentments I formed when my deepest beliefs and convictions were disparaged. And until this moment, I have rarely felt safe enough to reengage on contested issues.

Finally, I am between prevailing worldviews. Were forced choices demanded of me on a range of topics, there is no doubt that I would test out in the blue zone. But not in the end zone. I'd be much more likely to be between the sixty-yard lines. To mix metaphors, I am more likely to view policy choices as close calls than as layups. I am inclined to sit it out when the terms of discussion are stark and when the tone is shrill. I hate snark, ridicule, and schadenfreude, particularly when they come from those with whom I agree on the substance.

The Public Conversations Project's Carol Becker[1] has a brilliant take on this dynamic. She writes,

> Polarized public conversations can be described as conforming to a *dominant discourse*, . . . the most generally available and adopted way of discussing the issue in a public context. . . . Dominant discourses strongly influence which ideas, experiences, and observations are regarded as normal or eccentric, relevant or irrelevant. On a subject that has been hotly polarized for a long time, the dominant discourse often delineates the issue in a win-lose bi-polar way; it draws a line between two simple answers to a complex dilemma and induces people to take a stand on one side of that line or the other. . . . Most people who care deeply about the issue yield to this induction.

Becker continues,

> Being aligned with one group offers benefits. It gives one a socially validated place to stand . . . and it offers

---

[1] Carol Becker et al., "From Stuck Debate to New Conversation on Controversial Issues: A Report from the Public Conversations Project," www.publicconversations.org.

the unswerving support of like-minded people. It also exacts costs. . . . To be loyal to [one's] group, one must suppress many uncertainties, morally complicated personal experiences, inner value conflicts, and differences between oneself and one's allies. Complexity and authenticity are sacrificed to the demands of presenting a unified front to the opponent. A dominant discourse of antagonism is self-perpetuating. Win-lose exchanges create losers who feel they must retaliate to regain lost respect, integrity, and security, and winners who fear to lose disputed territory won at great cost.

What with polarized players finding each other virtually incomprehensible, even loathsome, reconciling voices are needed now more than ever. So I am left wondering: Are there safe places for such Catholics to engage on the pressing issues of the day without "yielding to the induction"?

I want to believe that those of us whose worldviews rarely fit into recognizable clusters have a role to play. I want to believe that we can reset the conversation and heal the wounds. But before we can deploy the bridging social capital we may uniquely possess, we must find one another. I hope that can begin today.

Part 2

Naming the Wounds

3
Polarized Preferences, Polarized Pews

Tricia C. Bruce

Two patterns shape American Catholics' contemporary churchgoing behavior. First, unlike their erstwhile pre–Vatican II counterparts, parishes now exhibit extraordinary distinctiveness, particularly when it comes to liturgy. The freedom to cater to local culture has enlivened parishes with individual personas. Territorial boundaries are no longer the primary distinguishing factor between parishes, traditional Latin liturgies no longer the shared routine. The enculturation and diversification fostered by Vatican II has birthed guitars, lay input, vernacular Scriptures, and popular styling—embraced and realized differently across Masses and across parishes. American parishes can look vastly different from one another.

Second, individual Catholics are ever more likely to choose a parish rather than to simply attend the one within whose territorial boundaries they reside. Catholics' parish choices pair convenience with individual identities and preferences for worship, ideology, special ministries, language, and so forth. Parishioners congregate less along the lines of shared neighborhood and more along the lines of shared preference, in a place that feels most at "home," geography notwithstanding. This trend cuts across religious denominations, as congregations move increasingly from ascription to achievement.[1]

In short: parish differences breed parish choices, and Catholics are choosing.

What is the effect of this partitioning? Catholic churches in the United States reflect what journalist Bill Bishop has called the "big sort," through which Americans are "reordering their lives around their values, their tastes, and their beliefs, . . . clustering in communities of like-mindedness."[2] Increased specialization has brought about "media, organizations, and associations that [are] both more segmented and more homogenous." The phenomenon reveals what sociologists call the homophily principle, or the tendency of people to live, work, and otherwise gather with those similarly situated.[3] Birds of a feather flock together.

Racial, socioeconomic, political, and educational differences—hardened to the extent that they overlap with shared neighborhoods—find their realization in Catholic parishes vastly apart in terms of race, class, politics, and education. Leaving aside the power differential that comes from such divisions, they are, on their very face, an exacerbation of a polarized America. Like other Americans, Catholics sort themselves according to their own social positioning. And this partitioning cannot be viewed in isolation—parish choices extend and exacerbate polarization happening in America more broadly.

Take, for example, the cases of Blessed Sacrament and St. Matthew's parishes (both pseudonyms), residing in two different dioceses and, arguably, in two different corners of the

---

[1] See Stephen R. Warner, "The Place of the Congregation in the Contemporary American Religious Configuration," *American Congregations* (1994): 54–99.

[2] Bill Bishop, *The Big Sort: Why the Clustering of Like-Minded America Is Tearing Us Apart* (New York: Houghton Mifflin Harcourt, 2009), 12, 37.

[3] Miller McPherson, Lynn Smith-Lovin, and James M. Cook, "Birds of a Feather: Homophily in Social Networks," *Annual Review of Sociology* (2001): 415–44.

Catholic imagination. Blessed Sacrament is nestled within a predominantly white, semi- to highly affluent suburban area of a Southern diocese. Its neighborhood matters little to its parishioner composition, however, because it is a Catholic parish with *no* territorial boundaries. Parishioners come to the church not because their residence falls within parish boundaries (there are none) but because the parish offers Mass exclusively in Latin.

Arriving in modest, muted attire, the faithful process in quietly to attend Blessed Sacrament's High Mass late Sunday mornings. They are greeted by a large crucifix in the vestibule and a worship area likewise assuming the shape of a cross. Women pin chapel veils atop their hair, borrowing from the foyer basket as needed. Men arrive in jackets and ties; children (of which there are many) mirror their parents' fashion. Were it not for the many youthful faces in the room—including that of the priest—one may conclude that Blessed Sacrament and its people have survived as a conservative relic of pre–Vatican II Catholicism, older Catholics gripping tightly to the Latin rite through a half-century of resistance. But no; this is not an antiquated base of Catholicism. It is a youthful and vibrant, albeit quiet, and highly traditional community that prefers a deliberately reverent liturgical form. Mass at Blessed Sacrament is celebrated according to the Roman Missal of 1962. The pastor belongs to a community of priests whose primary mission is to ordain and train men to celebrate the Traditional Latin Mass, deploying them to dioceses where their presence will be welcomed by a local bishop. Blessed Sacrament is a *personal parish* devoted to the Extraordinary Form of the Roman Rite.

Elsewhere—at St. Matthew's parish, in a Midwestern diocese—one encounters an impressive stockpile of clothing and household items on the curb most weekends, free for the taking. Residents from the parish's predominantly African American neighborhood depart with garbage bags filled with needed items. Here, too, boundaries do not apply: nearly all of

St. Matthew's parishioners drive in from elsewhere, electing by affinity to attend this Catholic parish explicitly devoted to social justice.

Mass at St. Matthew incorporates heavy lay involvement and an intentional welcome to "people of all ages and persuasions," as stated in the parish's mission. This is readily apparent in the hodgepodge of attendees and emotional messages delivered during the service, often by lay women. Prayers of the faithful, offered from the front as well as impromptu from the pews, welcome those hurt or marginalized by the church. "For all gay, lesbian, bisexual, and transgender individuals, especially young people, struggling with their identities, may they accept themselves and may the church accept them, coming to recognize their equality in Christ." A shared sign of peace drowns out the choir with rowdy handshakes and hugs across the aisle. Facing declining neighborhood attendees, St. Matthew's social justice personal parish designation warded off closure during diocesan restructuring a decade ago.

Considered together—though they may appear to stand far apart—Blessed Sacrament and St. Matthew reveal the polarized expressions of Catholicism embedded in parishes and made feasible amid a diverse Catholic Church. Both are canonical parishes. They are not fringe groups lacking formal status, though their approaches may resonate with those at or near the ideological edges of the church. Neither are they ex-Catholic or alternatively Catholic, lacking official recognition or rendered outsiders through formal dismissal (though these sorts of communities, too, dot the American landscape). No, Blessed Sacrament and St. Matthew are both canonical parishes. They are wholly a part of the respective dioceses they inhabit, wholly connected to the official Roman Catholic Church in the United States, and wholly illustrative of the kind of polarization that can rack American Catholics.

Personal Parishes

Personal parish status comes from an allowance in Canon Law empowering bishops to discern occasions when parishes can meet particular, otherwise unmet needs of niche populations of Catholics. Canon 518, from the 1983 Code of Canon Law, reads:

> As a general rule a parish is to be territorial, that is, one which includes all the Christian faithful of a certain territory. When it is expedient, however, personal parishes are to be established determined by reason of the rite, language, or nationality of the Christian faithful of some territory, or even for some other reason. (Can. 518)

Local bishops may discern when—and for whom or what—personal parishes can be established.

A notable side effect of this has been a modest but measurable increase in parishes devoted to particular ideological iterations of the faith or, in the more subdued language used by sociologist Nancy Ammerman to describe elective parochialism, differing "arenas of everyday practice."[4] But personal parishes are not merely "de facto congregations" that have adapted over time to an elective character born of parishioners' own affinities and facilitating pastors.[5] Rather, they are officially dedicated to a niche purpose.

Of course, American Catholic history boasts a long (albeit uneven) precedent for parishes with canonically decreed service to special groups: namely, minority ethnic, national, or linguistic groups. National parishes (now also subsumed under

---

[4] See Nancy T. Ammerman, *Congregation and Community* (New Brunswick, NJ: Rutgers University Press, 1997), 358. Data on the increase of personal parishes comes from a national study of personal parishes conducted by the author (Tricia C. Bruce) in Fall 2012. This material will be published in a forthcoming book with Oxford University Press.

[5] See Warner, "The Place of the Congregation in the Contemporary American Religious Configuration."

the personal parish label) have for more than a century served Polish, German, and Lithuanian Catholics and the like, and in more recent years, Vietnamese, Chinese, and Korean Catholics as well.[6] But what of parishes like Blessed Sacrament and St. Matthew, where the personal parish purpose is defined not by language, nationality, or ethnicity? Liturgical and pastoral preferences—arguably coterminous with ideological preferences—are what structures these sorts of personal parishes.

Though proportionately few among more than 17,000 US parishes, these personal parishes are nonetheless significant for formally combining Catholics not along territorial lines but the lines of identity. Personal parishes magnify through their creation the fissures reverberating along ideological lines throughout the US Catholic Church.[7] And they harken at core sociological questions of individualism, community, and the social solidarity that glues people together.

Personal parishes acknowledge—officially—differences among Catholics as parish-selecting parishioners and differences among parishes as havens for similarly situated Catholics. Here, polarization in the US church is not merely a subtle or accidental reality, accomplished only through the de facto practices of Mass-attending American Catholics. Status is made "de jure" through the canonical decree required for the erection of personal parishes. Personal parishes label a clear home for traditional Catholics, for social justice–oriented Catholics,

---

[6] The story of personal parishes for ethnocultural groups such as these has found livelihood through the work of Jay Dolan in *The Immigrant Church* (Notre Dame, IN: University of Notre Dame Press, 1983), Joseph Edward Ciesluk in *National Parishes in the United States* (Washington, DC: Catholic University of America Press, 1947), and Tricia Bruce, "Preserving Catholic Space and Place in 'The Rome of the West,'" in *Spiritualizing the City: Agency and Resilience of the Urbanesque Habitat*, ed. Victoria Hegner and Peter Jan Margry, Routledge Studies in Urbanism and the City (New York: Routledge, forthcoming), among others.

[7] See Mary Ellen Konieczny, *The Spirit's Tether: Family, Work, and Religion among American Catholics* (Oxford: Oxford University Press, 2013).

for Catholics of particular ethnic backgrounds, and so forth. Though personal parishes remain in the minority among all parishes, they nonetheless signify the real and symbolic lines that separate American Catholics.

Naming the problem of polarization in the Catholic Church means naming its occurrence writ large. Personal parishes name the problem of polarization in a real, codified way. Their official designations evoke canon law and originate only with a local bishop's approval. Personal parishes are decreed to be certain things to certain people. They partition Catholics in service of specialized needs. Whether or not this is problematic is a complicated question: there are often justifiable moral and pragmatic reasons to create personal parishes. But the effect is all the same: Catholics are polarized. The phenomenon of personal parishes insinuates three questions meriting deeper consideration for their impact on unity in the wider church. I discuss each in turn.

Are Personal Parishes Really "Parishes"?

First, "parish" denotes place. Roman Catholic polity is built upon a parish structure that divides dioceses into geographic units: parishes. Unlike other denominations whose congregations are autonomously owned, the polity undergirding Catholic parishes encourages a strong connection to the wider ecology in which it is embedded.[8] Territorial parishes are designed to serve all in their midst: "The parish is the presence of the church in a given territory," writes Pope Francis.[9] Bounded

---

[8] See John T. McGreevy, *Parish Boundaries: The Catholic Encounter with Race in the Twentieth-Century Urban North* (Chicago: The University of Chicago Press, 1998), and Gerald Gamm, *Urban Exodus: Why the Jews Left Boston and the Catholics Stayed* (Cambridge, MA: Harvard University Press, 2009).

[9] Francis, Apostolic Exhortation *Evangelii Gaudium* (On the Proclamation of the Gospel in Today's World), November 24, 2013, http://w2.vatican.va /content/francesco/en/apost_exhortations/documents/papa-francesco _esortazione-ap_20131124_evangelii-gaudium.html, 24.

catchment areas, moreover, end only when and where another begins, linking all to a wider web. Parishes do not exist in isolation (nor can they, canonically); parishes are like puzzle pieces within a larger diocesan landscape.

But at Blessed Sacrament or St. Matthew—and at their personal parish counterparts around the nation—this geographic "parish" connotation morphs into something that looks more congregational. Personal parishes need no geographic area; they draw worshipers from throughout a diocese and do not necessarily reach back out into the very neighborhoods in which they reside. They relegate this task to the geographic parish within whose boundaries their physical church technically resides. This may lessen parishioners' sense of neighborhood belonging or indebtedness to dissimilar others. As one pastor described, "There's no sense of me belonging to this geography anymore."

Personal parishes, as such, drive forms of community driven less by proximity and more by elected affinity. As social theorist Georg Simmel observed of space and community, "[B]oundary is not a spatial fact with sociological consequences, but a sociological fact that forms itself spatially."[10] Whereas territorial boundaries reify a diverse mixing of proximate Catholics, personal parishes enable detached and decentralized bodies of Catholics whose activities proceed independently of geographic location. Personal parishes sit in-between elective and ascribed parochialism.

Do Personal Parishes Reflect Failed Community?

Second, just as "parish" denotes place, it simultaneously denotes community. Per the Catechism (2179), "A parish is a definite community of the Christian faithful established on a stable basis within a particular church." Parishes bring Catholics together to foster and maintain communal bonds. They are among the

---

[10] See *Simmel on Culture*, ed. David Frisby and Mike Featherstone (London: Sage, 1997), 143.

few brick-and-mortar institutions designed to regularly foster meaningful in-person contact that cuts across lines of difference. Even to the extent that parishes tend toward homogeneity, "individualism and communalism are utterly intertwined."[11] As social theorist Emile Durkheim notes, religion's eminently social character unifies a moral community.

But while personal parishes, too, generate forms of community, their very existence presupposes that community is *not* being forged neatly—or at least evenly—among territorial parishes. Tensions often emerge in parishes hosting multiple niche communities of Catholics. Fellow parishioners don't always get along.[12] Liturgies, moreover, may even appear to be mutually exclusive. Says one pastor of a Traditional Latin Mass parish, "Even though they are different forms of the same rite, they're still very different. It's almost like a different world." This, of course, presumes that dissimilar Catholics are sharing a parish at all. The vast majority of parishes are already divided into homogenous communities as a consequence of residential and/or preferential patterns, leaving little opportunity for clashes across different groups. Catholics choose parishes; race, ethnicity, class, ideology, and taste congeal similar Catholics and sift out dissimilar ones.

Personal parishes can compensate for the marginalization of some communities in territorial parishes. Blessed Sacrament creates a safe haven for traditional Catholics; St. Matthew makes a home for more progressive Catholics. "That is just great," confides one Latin Mass attendee, "to be able to see that we're not outsiders. The ghettoizing of the Latin Mass has occurred in certain places, and no: we're part of the fabric of the diocese, which is just a great thing, the way it ought to be." As Karl Marx theorized some time ago, those who control the resources control the story: to the extent that marginalized Catholics never control the resources, a parish may never

---

[11] Ammerman, *Congregation and Community*, 353.

[12] See Brett C. Hoover, *The Shared Parish: Latinos, Anglos, and the Future of US Catholicism* (New York: NYU Press, 2014).

feel like one's own. Some remain outsiders to their ascribed territorial parish—unless or until they can become insiders as a personal parish.

Are Personal Parishes Facilitating Isolation?

Third, personal parishes isolate—contain, even—divergent expressions of Catholicism. Marked by a given orientation, personal parishes consolidate parishioners who share that orientation under a single, literal roof—and apart from others in the diocese. A narrow "we" delineates over and against an othered "they" in the church. Again, from Simmel, "It is as if each individual largely felt his own significance only by contrasting himself with others."[13] Catholics' differentiation produces factions within a shared church.

This kind of narrow isolation can reduce social contact and increase social distance. Interpersonal contact, absent to the extent that Catholics are physically attending parishes with others who think similarly, reduces opportunities to eliminate prejudice.[14] Regularly interacting only with those whose views you share can exacerbate social distance between you and a perceived "other." As Bill Bishop writes, "[T]he benefit that ought to come with having a variety of opinions is lost to the righteousness that is the special entitlement of homogeneous groups."[15]

Isolation and centralization in personal parishes, moreover, may be utilized by Catholic leaders as a means of managing diversity in a diocese. A pastoral leader at St. Matthew, for example, recollects how her bishop's decision to make St. Matthew

---

[13] See *The Sociology of Georg Simmel*, ed. and trans. Kurt H. Wolff (London: The Free Press of Glencoe, 1964), 31.

[14] Contact theory suggests that given the right conditions, including equitable status, interpersonal contact can reduce prejudice. The prior discussion of parishes as communities, however, may suggest that parish conditions are not always primed for meaningful contact across difference. See G. W. Allport, *The Nature of Prejudice* (Cambridge, MA: Perseus Books, 1954).

[15] See Bishop, *The Big Sort*, 14.

a personal parish seemed less about honoring their own perspectives as it was about—as she puts it—"keeping all the crazy folks in one spot so they can be contained." Indeed, one online observer deemed the community "an absolute embarrassment to every Catholic."

Bringing together like-minded Catholics can also consolidate priest and ministry resources: other parishes and priests need not cater to those special needs or different desires. Comments one leader, "There's something good about it, and there's something ill-conceived about it. I think that every parish should have a certain commitment to social justice, because we have a responsibility to do this. I don't think it's necessary to say, 'Well, let's send them all onto the ship and send them away.'" Another leader extols the capacity of personal parishes to reach otherwise excluded groups, warning nonetheless that "if [a personal parish] becomes an excuse to silo and strategically marginalize or contain that prophetic spirit, then I think we're not being very healthy, and it's a problem."

Such a critique finds parallel in comments offered by Pope Francis (2013):

> This is a danger: we shut ourselves up in the parish, with our friends, within the movement, with the like-minded. . . . [B]ut do you know what happens? When the Church becomes closed, she becomes an ailing Church, she falls ill! That is a danger. Nevertheless we lock ourselves up in our parish, among our friends, in our movement, with people who think as we do. . . . [B]ut do you know what happens? When the Church is closed, she falls sick, she falls sick. Think of a room that has been closed for a year. When you go into it there is a smell of damp, many things are wrong with it. A Church closed in on herself is the same, a sick Church.

In its most troublesome consequence, then, the isolating nature of personal parishes materializes itself not only in the polarization of a unified church but also in an unhealthy lack of dialogue and growth.

Apart . . . and Together

Personal parishes embed polarization into the very structures of local Catholicism. They are not just an ad hoc consequence of Catholics' choices, but a reality codified by local bishops' decision making and an accepted application of canon law. Personal parishes serve as both a real and symbolic representation of division in the US church.

While St. Matthew and Blessed Sacrament highlight divisions along the lines of liturgy and mission, divisions also name and separate Catholics along other lines. Individual Catholics' agency in choosing a parish where they feel most at home cannot be explained away by "preference." People desire different types of religious communities, to be sure. But "taste," as such, can also parade as a disguise for racial, class, and political divisions polarizing America and the broader Catholic Church. "Taste classifies," theorizes sociologist Pierre Bourdieu, "and it classifies the classifier."[16] Paired with a legitimation formally extended by an institutional authority—a parish officially serving only certain Catholics—these patterns merit especially careful attention.

But ending the discussion here would unfairly—or at least incompletely—conclude that personal parishes are, in and of themselves, a polarizing problem among American Catholics. This conclusion presumes that when we look for diversification and unity, we look at each American Catholic parish on its own. But Catholic parishes do not stand alone. They are linked to authority structures that are far from autonomous. They coexist alongside other personal parishes and territorial parishes, embedded in transparish networks within and across

---

[16] See Pierre Bourdieu, *Distinction: A Social Critique of the Judgement of Taste* (Abingdon, Oxon: Routledge, 2013), xxix. Bourdieu further describes the notion of shared "habitus" produced from common class standing, generating in turn common structures and common notions of what counts as common-sense. See Bourdieu, *The Logic of Practice* (Stanford, CA: Stanford University Press, 1990).

dioceses. Parish communities necessarily reside within wider communities of Catholics.

This vantage point—the forest, rather than the trees—can lend a different conclusion. Personal parishes are specialist organizations. Our litmus test for religious vitality and unity ought not to stop at the level of individual congregations. Unity cuts across the church in its entirety. While it is useful to analyze solidarity and integration in individual parishes, this must be paired with a view toward solidarity and integration in the full US church. This is all the more true for Catholicism, given its enduring parochial structure. Specialization breeds its own style of solidarity: interdependence.

Seen in this light, personal parishes may bring as much hope as they do derision. They can offer a home for Catholics otherwise "homeless" or insufficiently welcomed in the church. They are parishes; they are communities. Personal parishes—in naming a safe haven for certain Catholics—generate needed spaces of inclusion. Parish pews are filled with Catholics whose love for the church integrates seamlessly with other meaningful personal identities, reviving and sustaining American Catholics' faith and communal commitments. Individual preferences and shared bonds are ultimately interdependent: the existence of one presupposes that of the other.

The final question is thus: can these two narratives coexist? Can personal parishes polarize the church while simultaneously bonding and integrating like-minded Catholics? I would posit that yes, even in the face of complexity and potential contradiction, personal parishes can do both. Differences exist among Catholics; parishes turn these differences into structural realities. Viewed in isolation, this is a polarizing problem to be resolved. Viewed in union across a wider church, this is a mosaic to be celebrated.

4

Whither Polarization?
(Non) Polarization on the Ground

Susan Crawford Sullivan

I remember when I first learned of polarization in the Catholic Church. I was thirty-two, a first-year PhD student, and lifelong Catholic. I had worked for Catholic Charities, attended parish retreats, and helped lead youth ministry in one of my parishes for a time, but I was still pretty fully (looking back unbelievably, inexplicably) in the dark about polarization in the Catholic Church. I was attending a weeklong conference on Catholic intellectual life for faculty at Catholic colleges and universities. A few graduate students interested in teaching at Catholic colleges and universities were also invited to attend, and so there I was. As it turned out, some of the attendees were displeased by the choice of speakers, finding them too "liberal." Debates raged among our small discussion groups. At one point, someone turned to me and said, "Are you a liberal or a conservative Catholic?" I simply stared at them, rather stumped by the question. I had honestly never thought before how I should categorize myself, or even that these categories existed. "I don't know," I finally replied. "I'm just a suburban Catholic."

Looking back, even I find this hard to believe, given what I know now about polarization in the church. "Just a suburban Catholic." Yet I would suspect that many of my highly involved fellow parishioners in my current parish might reply much the same.

I grew up in the 1970s and 1980s in suburban neighborhood-based, family-oriented parishes. We went to Mass on Saturday evenings, where my dad was the organist. My parents (mostly my dad) were involved in the movements of the era—Cursillo, the Charismatic Movement, Renew. In one parish, my mother learned a few chords on the guitar to play in the folk Mass. In a later parish in another state, she helped run the parish craft bazaar. One of our priests there was legendary for his speedy Masses on Sundays when the Redskins were playing. There were no evident deep ideological interests, much less polarizations. College (at a non-Catholic school) was mostly just Mass on Sunday night. After college, living in Hawaii, I became very involved in another family-centered, geographically centered parish, getting to know the pastor well and volunteering in youth ministry. Again, no evident polarization in the parish or strong polarized ideologies—parish life was focused on the excellent Hawaiian choir and the dynamic youth ministry.

Detour through graduate school, an urban university parish, lots of reading, and engagement with Catholic intellectual life—and I now know more about polarization in the church than I would have ever wanted to know. Over the years, I've read the gamut of Catholic publications: *America* and *First Things*, *National Catholic Register* and *National Catholic Reporter*. Yet I am raising my children in the moderate, nonpolarized neighborhood parish across the street from my house, a large suburban parish focused on family life. It is somewhat of a disconnect, being involved in Catholic intellectual life yet making a parish home where Catholic intellectual and political concerns barely register. My husband's and my four children attend the parish school, and many of our closest friends are from the parish. Our friends and fellow parishioners, mostly college-educated professionals, don't read the *National Catholic Reporter* or *National Catholic Register*. I doubt most know that either publication exists. They don't read *First Things* or *Commonweal* or *America* and likely have never heard of them. A few friends sometimes catch a show on EWTN because it's on in our area, but most don't see it as part of "conservative" Catholicism—they see it as just the Catholic TV channel. Largely, parish life—outside of the celebration of the Mass—revolves around family activities, parish school activities, coffee hours, religious education, and so on. People sign up for the service day to help the poor in our area and donate to our sister parish in Haiti. People recite "Lord hear our prayer," when the prayer of the faithful asks us to pray for all of human life from conception to natural death; this is accepted as part of Catholic tradition and seemingly provokes no polarization. The parish is full of two- and three-child families, so I suspect that like most American Catholics, most parishioners choose not to accept the birth control teaching. I honestly could not say how most people feel about other contested political issues (for example, gay marriage) or Catholic issues (such as female priests, married priests), because these issues do not come up, at least not in ways that I have seen in ten years of involvement there.

I have to imagine that a good number of American Catholics find parish life to be this way. Data from the National Congregations Study, for example, shows that the largest number of the almost nine hundred Catholic parishes responding to survey questions (almost 50 percent) describe themselves as theologically and politically "right in the middle."[1] General Social Survey data from 2010 show 36 percent of Catholics self-identifying as "moderate," 25 percent as "traditional," 21 percent as "liberal," and 18 percent as "none of the above."[2] Brian Starks's 2013 qualitative research[3] finds that Catholics who self-identify as "moderate" most often believe themselves to hold a mix of liberal and conservative views and often em-

---

[1] I gratefully acknowledge the assistance of Linda Kawentel with National Congregations Study data.

[2] Brian Starks, "Exploring Religious Self-Identification among U.S. Catholics: Traditionals, Moderates, and Liberals," *Sociology of Religion* 74, no. 3 (2013): 314–42.

[3] Ibid.

phasize that they do not hold extreme positions. Starks's research finds "moderate" Catholics to be pragmatic and focused on local parish life, as expressed by one of his interviewees: "[I]t's more about right here and now today; getting ready for the festival, taking people to the doctor when their kids can't do it. . . . Real world Catholics, I think, are moderate."[4] By contrast, self-identified "liberal" and "traditional" Catholics in Starks's study believed moderate Catholics to be indifferent, uninterested, or apathetic, ascribing to them no clear identity or agenda.

While Mary Ellen Konieczny in *The Spirit's Tether* shows Catholics "on the ground" who participate in either strongly liberal or conservative parishes which might fuel polarization, many Catholics probably experience parish life far from the ideological issues that rend the church. Other chapters in this volume likewise name the "wounds" of polarization. But this chapter speaks less of wounds than of lack of knowledge or engagement in the polarizing issues of the broader church.[5] Whether this is a "wound" can be debated, although it obviously can have downsides. In a more optimistic tone, this chapter examines intentionality and strategic deterrence of polarization on the ground, allowing the development of a welcoming and active parish culture.

The fact that many American Catholics are living out their faith in moderate parishes, more or less removed from strong ideological identities, raises several questions. One is how such parishes come about. Moderate, nonpolarized parishes may come about through a variety of factors: a preponderance of theologically moderate people in a parish—perhaps self-selecting

[4] Ibid., 338.

[5] Christian Smith and colleagues claim that many American Catholics younger than the Vatican II generation are not very knowledgeable about the Catholic faith. See Christian Smith, Kyle Longest, Jonathan Hill, and Kari Christoffersen, *Young Catholic America: Emerging Adults In, Out of, and Gone from the Church* (Oxford and New York: Oxford University Press, 2014).

into it, perhaps from a lack of knowledge or desire for engagement in certain issues among parishioners, perhaps due to intentional pastoral strategies or other reasons. A second question involves what we can learn from these parishes that might be useful when considering polarization in the church more broadly. Are there lessons that might be helpful? And a third question considers the potential downsides of such parishes, examining their limitations. In reflecting on these questions, I provide a case study relying on participation observation and data from an in-depth interview with the pastor of a moderate parish with a nonpolarizing culture.

Framing Polarization

I first frame the polarization debate by drawing on the useful discussion of the topic provided by Mary Ellen Konieczny in the introduction to her excellent book *The Spirit's Tether: Family, Work, and Culture among American Catholics*. In a 1991 book aptly titled *Culture Wars*, James Davidson Hunter argued that the United States had become increasingly polarized in recent decades in matters ranging from politics to the family. According to Hunter, religion played into and fueled these debates, with splits between religious liberals and religious conservatives. Scholars such as Paul DiMaggio and Alan Wolfe disagreed, drawing on opinion data that showed that Americans were not polarized on most issues; these critics claimed that culture wars existed among elites, not ordinary Americans. More recently, Robert Putnam and David Campbell used survey data to argue that moral polarization does indeed exist outside of elites, but they focus on the split between religious and secular Americans.[6]

---

[6] See Mary Ellen Konieczny, *The Spirit's Tether: Family, Work, and Religion among American Catholics* (Oxford and New York: Oxford University Press, 2013), 4–5. Works she reviews include James Davidson Hunter, *Culture Wars: The Struggle to Define America* (New York: Basic Books, 1991); Paul DiMaggio,

Konieczny steps usefully into this debate by drawing attention to differences among religious Americans, Catholics in this case, and by focusing on polarizing issues related to the family. In order to generate better understanding of how religion fuels ordinary Americans' moral polarization, Konieczny studies two Catholic parishes chosen to represent "ideal types"—one conservative, or orthodox, and the other liberal, or progressive. Members of these parishes are drawn from similar demographics: both parishes attract a large number of mostly white, highly educated professionals as parishioners—doctors, lawyers, teachers, business managers—the Catholic middle and upper middle classes. The parishioners studied, however, also represent particular chosen or achieved Catholic identities. They reflect Catholic participation in a culture of religious choice that has been well-documented and debated by other scholars.[7]

Many of the parishioners Konieczny studied seem to have chosen parishes (liberal or conservative) which resonate with their own values and views on Catholicism. For some, parish participation further shapes their religious identity; for others, participation allows for a continuation of identity. Participation in these parishes reinforces and deepens a sense of polarization, with the bonding and belonging to their community (with its particular orientation to Catholicism) defined against others, particularly other Catholics. Moral boundaries are drawn against other types of Catholics in areas such as work and family decisions, contraception, marriage, motherhood and fatherhood, as well as in religious issues like worship style.

John Evans, and Bethany Bryson, "Have American's Social Attitudes Become More Polarized?," *American Journal of Sociology* 102, no. 3 (November 1996): 690–755; Alan Wolfe, *One Nation, After All* (New York: Penguin Books), 1999; Robert D. Putnam and David E. Campbell, *American Grace: How Religion Divides and Unites Us* (New York: Simon & Schuster, 2010).

[7] See Konieczny, *The Spirit's Tether*, 240–44, for a discussion of some of the research on religious choice and the impact of religious choice on American Catholicism.

Konieczny claims that it is in congregations that "local-level polarization processes" around religion and the family are most likely to be found and shows through analysis of case studies what "cultural processes sustain polarizing processes within them."[8] Konieczny does state that her case studies were chosen to represent ideal types and says that most American parishes are more middle of the road. The book ends by calling for future research that studies parishes that resist polarization or creatively accommodate polar views.

I contend that many Americans do indeed worship in spaces that either resist polarization or find ways to accommodate polarized views. Here I present a case study of one such parish. Note, however, that these parishes can come about in a number of different ways. It is one task to take a group of well-informed Catholics with strongly held but different polar views and meld them into a functioning community that accommodates strongly held divergent views; it is another task to work with a parish composed largely of Catholics who perhaps have relatively little awareness of or immersion in the issues and language of polarization in the church. In this essay, I will discuss the latter.

Case Study

The pastor of the case study New England parish has been a diocesan priest for over twenty-five years, with considerable experience around the diocese and a good knowledge of parishes outside of his current one, where he has served for ten years. While general conclusions cannot be drawn from one case study, this case does offer insight into how some parishes that resist polarization or polarized identities come into being and operate.

The parish under consideration, which I will call Saint Therese (a pseudonym), is a large parish in a middle-class and upper middle-class Massachusetts suburban town. It is a geo-

---

[8] See Mary Ellen Konieczny's introduction to this volume, p. ix.

graphically based parish, and most parishioners live in the town, where it is the larger of two Catholic parishes. The parish consists of 2800 households, with 1300 of those considered active households. There is a parish school of more than two hundred children, and there are one thousand public school children in grades one to ten enrolled in religious education, with one hundred volunteer CCD teachers. In the past year, there were approximately one hundred baptisms, 130 First Communions, 110 Confirmations, six weddings, and seventy funerals. There are numerous social activities: a large multiday family festival, Lenten fish fry, pasta festival, Christmas craft fair, annual pub quiz, and more. There are also a number of social activities and a morning Bible study for older parishioners. The parish has a parish nurse, and there are exercise classes for older congregants. Adult education opportunities are provided in the form of occasional study groups and mission speakers. A mom's spirituality group, men's group, and couples' ministry all attract small numbers. Primary parish activities take place through the main ministries, which are intergenerational and whose active leadership consists of about one hundred members. There are eight main ministries: Stewardship, Liturgy, Health and Bereavement, Respect Life, Social Justice, Outreach, Community, and Education.

Prior to an in-depth interview with the pastor, I had assumed that the moderate, nonpolarized nature of this parish came about due to the composition of its members. The parish is located in a politically moderate town split evenly between Democrats and Republicans, in a Democratic state that often elects Republican governors and where highly polarized political movements like the Tea Party hold little traction. The parishioners are mostly suburban families seeking a church upbringing for their children, as well as senior citizens who have already raised their families in the parish. The demographic is primarily white, with a growing number of Asian and African immigrant families. People are middle-class and upper middle-class professionals: doctors, lawyers, teachers, engineers, firefighters, police, nurses, etc. The parish demographic matches the town in which it is located, where most of its parishioners reside. The parish's climate would seem to arise from parishioners' mix of political moderation and busy suburban lifestyles focused on careers and family.

Upon interviewing the pastor, however, I discovered how much leadership and intentionality has gone into creating a moderate and nonpolarized Catholic parish. The pastor puts considerable thought and work into maintaining an environment welcoming of everyone and dealing with the small factions of people most likely to become polarizing. For example, when the pastor arrived ten years ago, the small pro-life ministry (Respect Life) was organizationally located within the Social Justice ministry. Respect Life was dissatisfied with this situation, so the pastor made them a main ministry, at an equivalent level to the Social Justice ministry. This made them feel like their mission was accorded equal respect and voice in the parish organizational structure.

The pastor has also guided the Respect Life ministry to present their mission to engage the larger parish community in nonpolarizing ways. When the ministry suggests activities to the pastor that he feels would fuel potential polarization, he asks them to reframe the activity in a less potentially polarizing way. Now, each year, the Respect Life asks the parish community to take home and fill up baby bottles with spare change to bring back and donate to a local organization that houses pregnant women in need of shelter. This is an activity that families are eager to participate in, and the parish children love taking the baby bottles home and doing chores or good deeds around the home to fill them with change. While the members of the small Respect Life community themselves participate in other activities such as regularly praying the rosary in front of a Planned Parenthood in a nearby city, these activities are not central (nor even very visible) to the broader parish community. Other social services and fundraising for the poor (for example, supporting a parish in Haiti) are activities that everyone can engage in; Pope Francis's emphasis on the poor makes this even more the case. Nonpolarized congregations focus on welcoming social events to provide a sense of community.

The pastor revealed other strategies for defusing potential polarization. He takes care to ensure that his homilies focus on the Scriptures. The homilies unpack the readings, look at Jesus's actions in the Gospel, and do not comment on political issues. When he receives mailings or a letter to the parish from the bishop about a political issue (for example, the bishop sent a letter to all parishes regarding an assisted suicide referendum), the pastor does not read these letters out loud or discuss their content from the pulpit but lets the congregation know that the bishop has sent a letter on the topic and that people can pick up a copy from a table near the entry if they would like. He exercises considerable pastoral judgment in determining how to implement diocesan material within this particular local context. Thus, pastoral leadership—and concordant lay leadership—matters tremendously in creating a nonpolarized parish. A moderate, nonpolarized parish needs leaders who are moderate, nonpolarizing, and committed to developing and maintaining an environment where people are broadly welcomed.

The fact that there are relatively small numbers of people likely to identify as strongly liberal or strongly conservative Catholics also contributes to a nonpolarizing climate. In the case study, both the Social Justice ministry and the Respect Life ministry (people who perhaps have the potential to hold the most polarized views) are composed of very small numbers of members, relative to the large parish. Few parishioners demonstrate strong polar views in this large suburban parish. Many are there for a church upbringing for their children and for the religious education program. Most members from the town come because the parish is nearby, not because they are seeking a particular orthodox or progressive community. Even without large numbers of parishioners likely to hold polarized views, pastoral intent strongly contributes to a nonpolarized parish identity by creating a space where everyone can feel welcome.

The Uninformed American Catholic?

I suspect that the parish considered in the case study represents the majority of such parishes: that is, they are composed of a pastor and a large number of parishioners who do not hold strong polarizing Catholic ideologies. Christian Smith argues in this volume that "Catholic polarization presupposes minimum levels of investment, commitment, and knowledge for such polarizing conflicts to make sense and be worth fighting over."[9] One obvious downside of the type of parish depicted by my case study is that moderate, family-oriented parishes may be largely composed of relatively uninformed Catholics. There are two types of polarization, often overlapping: political (issues such as abortion and gay marriage); and theological (such as the role of the magisterium or debates about women priests). But as Christian Smith and colleagues argue in *Young Catholic America: Emerging Adults In, Out of, and Gone From the Church*, Millennial generation American Catholics are not knowledgeable about the Catholic faith, in part due to the poor catechesis and knowledge of their own parents.[10] In this volume, Smith contends that very few Millennial generation Catholics are interested in or knowledgeable about polarizing issues in the church, and only a minority of Generation X Catholics are informed, interested, and vested in such issues.[11]

In other words, many Catholics likely do not hold polarized views on theological matters because they may not know enough to. It is well-documented that most American Catholics "make up their own minds" without taking church teaching

---

[9] See Christian Smith's reflection in this volume, p. 16.

[10] Smith et al., *Young Catholic America*.

[11] See p. 16 of this volume for Christian Smith's reflections on this.

into regard. It is surely a downside that parishes are not polarized because even very involved parishioners are not particularly knowledgeable about the Catholic faith. Surely the way to cure polarization is not to have a place where few people have serious knowledge or interest in broader issues of the church.

A related downside in such parishes is a lack of deep conversation around potentially polarizing issues. The small number of people likely to hold more polarizing views stay within their respective circles and ministries; the other large majority of people appear wholly disengaged from polarizing issues. As in any congregation catering to busy suburban families, members are stretched for time between parents' careers and children's numerous sports and other extracurricular activities. One might imagine a lecture series with discussion sessions on ideologically polarizing issues (the Supreme Court's decision legalizing gay marriage and what it might mean for the church; Pope Francis's teachings on economic inequality or the environment)—but people would likely feel too busy to attend, presuming they were even interested. Or, in a more positive interpretation, busy families choose to prioritize community building through parish social activities and children's religious education over deepening their knowledge of and engagement with polarizing theological and political issues in the Catholic Church.

Conclusion

I have offered preliminary observations and thoughts on an issue that calls out for more systematic study. Amid the conversation about polarization in the Catholic Church, it is worth noting that most American Catholics probably do not worship in ideologically polarized parishes in either direction. If many Americans worship in parishes that are nonpolarized spaces, then we should know more about how such spaces come to exist, what strengths such parishes have that can inform the broader discussion, and what downsides these parishes might have. Moderate, nonpolarized parishes can provide a strong sense of community for families to raise their children and live out their Catholic faith; such parishes, however, are not without their limitations. In any case, as the environments where large numbers of American Catholics live out their faith, they deserve further attention. The case study considered in this essay points to some clear pastoral strategies that aid in developing parishes that lessen or avoid polarization. The essay also points to disconnects between Catholics on the ground and (polarized) Catholic conversations in academia and media circles. Both of these issues merit further study in a consideration of polarization in the Catholic Church.

5

Ecclesial Inflammation
and LGBTQ Catholic Experiences

Brian P. Flanagan

My charge in this chapter is to name some of the wounds in the US Catholic Church opened by the phenomenon of openly lesbian, gay, bisexual, transgender, and queer persons. That is an awkward way of phrasing it—intentionally so, at least in part—but one that attempts to respect both the self-naming of persons who experience their sexuality in ways that do not fit traditional heterosexual paradigms while not limiting the woundedness to those who might self-identify as "queer," as "struggling with same-sex attraction," or, most commonly, as "lesbian, gay, or bisexual," and/or as "transgender."[1] Naming

---

[1] There is a currently much debate in many quarters about the joining together of the question of sexual orientation, that is, the gender to which one is attracted, with issues of gender identity. Historically, the connection begins with the shared experience of discrimination and violence against those perceived as "queer" in either their orientation, their gender identity, or both, but some advocates, both LGB and transgender, argue that the linking of these questions conflates two very different issues and even marginalizes the distinctiveness of transgender experience as an afterthought to identities rooted in sexual orientation. This is further complicated by the fact that within Roman Catholic magisterial teaching, there have been many interventions regarding same-sex sexual activity, but very few statements or clarifications with regard to gender identity and transgender persons. In this essay, I attempt

the experiences of LGBTQ people, of their families of origin and choice, and, for our purposes today, of their sisters and brothers in Christ, will not of itself "heal" any wounds, but naming the many varieties of that pain is crucial to beginning our conversation.

Two caveats are necessary with regard to my reflections. The first regards my qualifications. I am not a moral theologian or an ethicist, so my starting point for viewing these issues will not be the particular questions of the morality of same-sex sexual activity or same-sex marriage. I have opinions and biases on these questions, as we all do, but they are those of a Christian attempting to live out his baptism rather than those of a moral theologian specializing in the particular question of the morality of same-sex sexual activity. Instead, I am a systematic theologian and so will be addressing these questions as such. More specifically, I am an ecclesiologist, and so my questions revolve around the nature and identity of the church in relation to our grappling with the complexities of LGBTQ peoples' lives. How ought the church respond to the *novum* of openly lesbian and gay people in our world and in our parishes? How do its modes of response hamper or help its mission to be a foretaste of the reign of God in history, to promote, as Neil Ormerod names the mission of the church, "the prolongation of the healing vector of divine graciousness inaugurated by the Son and Spirit into human history"[2] in this moment? James Alison succinctly yet helpfully has written about "the gay thing" in human history, a shortened way of emphasizing that this is not only a question for people who

---

to mirror the "wide tent" approach of much of the contemporary queer community while acknowledging that the starting point of my reflections on ecclesial pain focus primarily on issues of sexual orientation and same-sex sexual activity, since it is with regard to these questions that the teaching authorities of the Catholic Church have been most vocal.

[2] Neil Ormerod, *Re-Visioning the Church: An Experiment in Systematic-Historical Ecclesiology* (Minneapolis: Fortress Press, 2014), 113.

self-identify as queer—rather, this is a question for us all inasmuch as we are sisters and brothers in Christ.[3] How the Body of Christ responds to this new social reality, then, is not simply a question of morality or policy but of our identity as a people.

My second caveat regards the limitations of a single voice. It would be foolish to expect one person to capture the many and varied ways that we all have been wounded in relationship to these issues. Unlike some of the contributors to this volume, I am not a sociologist, and so my data is less systematically collected. Nevertheless, while anecdotes make a shaky foundation for critical judgment, representative stories open up the imagination in ways that might help us enter into this conversation with some of the real people and complex situations that face us in our church today. And these particular stories open us up to the liturgical practices of lament, as theorized by Brad Hinze, among others.[4]

I'd like to begin by invoking some of the varied experiences of pain one could find in almost any Catholic parish, college, or family in the United States in 2015, not to rank people's pain, but to raise our imagination to how inflamed the Body of Christ is in relation to LGBTQ issues. These are some of the experiences of our sisters and brothers in Christ:

There is the pain of the devout Catholic teenager who finds himself confused and alarmed in discovering himself to have romantic and sexual attractions that differ from those of the majority of his classmates and finds himself alone, cut off in his shame from the communities of support that would assist him in almost any other trauma of his young life. This is, in some ways, the classic example, and I think we will be unable to really address the realities of queer people without a phenomenology of the closet. But as foundational, and often

---

[3] See, for instance, James Alison, "The Fulcrum of Discovery or: How the 'Gay Thing' Is Good News for the Catholic Church," www.jamesalison.co.uk.

[4] Bradford Hinze, "Ecclesial Impasse: What Can We Learn from Our Laments?," *Theological Studies* 72 (2011): 470–95.

still largely hidden, as these experiences are, there are other experiences of pain to which we need to attend.

There is the pain of the mother who finds herself torn between wanting to be faithful to the teachings of the Catholic Church on same-sex sexual activity while wanting to comfort, understand, and protect her lesbian daughter, a mother who winces every time she hears the phrase "objectively disordered" as a reference to her child.

There is the pain of the man who struggles with his feelings of same-sex attraction and wonders why a good God would give him such a cross to bear.

There is the pain of the college student who drifts away from the Catholic Church because the church's condemnation of her best friend seems to conflict the Gospel of mercy and justice with which she was raised.

There is the pain of the father who refuses to acknowledge his son's husband out of fidelity to the Catholic Church but finds himself increasingly cut off from the life of his son and his son's children, his grandchildren.

There is the pain of the transgender man whose experience and past journey are so incomprehensible to most of his fellow Catholics that every encounter within his local parish holds out the possibility of further incomprehension, disgust, or worse.

There is the pain of the Catholic woman and blogger whose honest attempt to be true to her faith and to express compassion for LGB people gets her called intolerant and a bigot by some and dangerously heterodox by others.

There is the pain of the gay man who, consciously or not, pushed aside his sexuality decades ago and found a way to serve Christ and Christ's church as a priest or brother, yet fears the implications of a world and a church that is very different from the one in which he was ordained.

There is the pain of the gay man of the same generation who chose differently, came out, saw his closest friends die from AIDS while the church stood at a distance and still harbors a deep bitterness toward the church of his youth and those who represent it.

There is the pain of the self-identified gay Catholic woman who has embraced celibacy to live out her sexuality but finds herself misunderstood and unwelcome in both the mainstream LGBT community and in the church to which she is giving herself.

There is the pain of the father of a gay man whose experience of the love in his son's life, on the one hand, and what, on the other, he hears from the pulpit of his parish, contrast so sharply that he questions whether the church has ever had anything true to say.

Finally, but no less importantly, there is the pain of many whose communion in Christ has been weakened, polarized, undermined, or broken due to our differing opinions and decisions on how to respond to these new experiences, challenges, ways of life. This is the pain of we who have been less than the *ecclesia* of God because of these differences.

There is pain.

I've used these examples and not others because I know, or have known, all of these people. The reader is also likely to have experience, known or unknown, of these stories. More radically, all of us are, by our shared baptism, in communion with the people behind these stories and the tens of thousands of other Catholic Christians who could tell similar stories. Focusing only on LGBT issues ignores, for the moment, all of the other intersections of pain in these people's lives; this litany also scandalously ignores the many moments of real joy and grace in these lives and lives like these. But for a conversation about polarization and woundedness in our church, this refrain needs to be the starting point—that whatever our opinions on the morality of same-sex sexual activity, gay marriage, ecclesial policy, or nondiscrimination acts, there is the pain, the pain of real people struggling in their love of God, of themselves, of their friends and family, and of God's church as we all come to awareness of the complexity of sexuality and gender identity in today's world. James Alison compares the adventure of our time in relation to the "gay thing" to a roller coaster ride, a ride in which he finds a great deal of joy, even a "sense of fun," in his words. This may be an important aspect of the experience—but the bruises caused by a rather rough ride need to be a part of our interpretation of the experience.

Furthermore, this pain is both very personal and very ecclesial—note how many of these experiences and stories involve the undermining, weakening, questioning, or breaking of relationships. Many of these stories involve the deep question of who belongs to the family, questions of whether I am/we are/they are part of the church or not. Before we talk about the issue of ecclesial polarization, the meta-pain that we all share and are focusing on in this volume, we need to see that these places of pain show us where the church is not yet the reconciled and reconciling Body of Christ, where our social relations remain insufficiently graced, insufficiently healed by the Holy Spirit. And that means that in the eschatological tension of the church's life, our ecclesial relations are not yet what they are called to be.

So, what kind of pain is this? Let me be autobiographical for a moment. I recently suffered a herniated disc in my lower back and learned a lot about the strength of our immune system's inflammatory response. The real pain—the sciatica, the numbness in my feet, the stabbing feeling in my back—came not only or primarily from the bones and the disc material but also from the acute inflammation that arose from the injury. "The inflammatory response," one can read in the Encyclopedia Britannica, "is a defense mechanism that evolved in higher organisms to protect them from infection and injury. Its purpose is to localize and eliminate the injurious agent and to remove damaged tissue components so that the body can begin to heal."[5] But even as a defense mechanism, acute in-

---

[5] Encyclopedia Britannica Online, s.v. "inflammation," accessed February 17, 2016, http://www.britannica.com/science/inflammation.

flammation *hurts*—it aches, it makes it difficult to be touched, it restricts one's range of motion, it can extend into previously unaffected regions of the body, drawing them into its field of nervous reaction, and it can shoot up in unexpected ways and times. What is primarily a protective process to respond to an injury or to an infection has immediate and practical consequences for one's body, one's mental state, and one's quality of life.

To continue with the classic corporeal metaphor of the church as the Body of Christ, our varying experiences of "the gay thing" have caused a great deal of acute inflammation in the Body. The experiences of our church regarding LGBTQ people, the varieties of pain we have felt, have made this a very tender ecclesial area. The narratives of pain I chronicled earlier have radiated out into many different parts of our church—to our families, to our parishes, to our institutions, and to our political lives. It has restricted our "range of motion"—our ability to credibly preach the Gospel and to make Christ present in a world that needs him and us. And what is particularly frustrating about the pain of inflammation is that even attempts to treat it can easily cause additional pain. How do we respond to a situation of pain in our church when many honest efforts seem to unintentionally do more harm than good?

My strongest hesitation in using this analogy is the danger of even using the language of "infection" in relation to LGBT issues, since the discourse of disease, contamination, impurity, cure, and "objective disorder" has such a long and negative history in relation to same-sex sexuality. But let me return briefly to the encyclopedia to note that inflammation is not always the result of direct infection or injury; "in other cases an inappropriate immune response may give rise to a prolonged and damaging inflammatory response. Examples include allergic, or hypersensitivity, reactions, in which an environmental agent such as pollen, which normally poses no threat to the individual, stimulates inflammation." Is the *novum* of new understandings of sexual orientation and gender identity in our world and times an infection, potentially harmful to the Body of Christ and needing to be excised, or is it more like the encounter with a new kind of pollen, triggering an allergic or autoimmune response? My hunch, something only to be further explored in coming years as the church continues to reflect our new awareness of sexual and gender diversity, is that the latter model is more accurate to the last fifty years of Catholic history—that "an inappropriate immune response" to the new reality of openly LGBT people in our church and society has given rise "to a prolonged and damaging inflammatory response."

That's a diagnosis better left to the moral theologians and the teachers of the church, but the *sensus fidei* of the church in the United States seems to provide some support for seeing our current situation more as an allergic reaction to a new substance rather than an appropriate reaction to a pathogen.

My point, therefore, is to bring to awareness the fact of long-term, damaging LGBT-related inflammation as a fact of our current life as the Body of Christ. But if we continue with my increasingly limping analogy, what model of healing are we going to use to address our inflammation? Do we need an anesthetic, an anti-inflammatory, physical therapy, or strategies for responding to chronic pain? In his book studying the liturgies for sickness, dying, and death, *Divine Worship and Human Healing*, Bruce Morrill raises the distinction between "curing" and "healing," distinguishing a late modern biomedical model of health from some pre- and postmodern understandings of healing. He writes,

> "Cure" refers to the effective control or removal of the disease in a person's body. "Healing," on the other hand, is an intervention affecting an illness. To heal somebody is to bring personal or social meaning to the misfortune experienced in illness such that the person attains a new or renewed sense of value and purpose in his or her world.[6]

---

[6] Bruce Morrill, *Divine Worship and Human Healing* (Collegeville, MN: Liturgical Press, 2009), 75.

Elsewhere he writes, in contrast to a biomedical model of a quick fix or miracle drug, "Healing is a matter of transforming people's perceptions of a critical or painful situation by making it somehow meaningful."[7] My plea, then, for our continuing conversation, is to ask how healing the Body of Christ from our LGBT-related inflammation is going to need to involve not simply a cure, not simply removing the pathogen or the antigen or coming to immediate and explicit agreement on how we should respond to LGB sexualities and transgender identity. It's not going to mean ignoring, minimizing, or, in the future, forgetting this moment of ecclesial pain but attempting to find meaning in this experience of pain through relation to the paschal mystery.

This is one of the test cases for the church in our time, not only for the sake of queer Catholics and their families but also because by practicing how to better be the reconciled and reconciling Body of Christ in this moment, we can grow in our skill in responding to future instances of ecclesial inflammation. Learning how to share communion while we disagree over LGBTQ issues is important for responding directly to the needs of LGBTQ Catholics. And it is important to be a sacrament for our divided world, now and in the future, such that unity in Christ is strong enough to bear our disagreements.

I end on a note of hope in the midst of pain. In his rich opening to a phenomenology and theology of lamentation in ecclesial experience, Bradford Hinze writes that "lament provides a process of purification on the way to a deeper wisdom about God, self, community, and others,"[8] and that to reach that wisdom requires deep, careful listening to lament and generous discernment of their spirit. In recent years, especially given the doors to dialogue pushed open by Pope Francis, awareness of ecclesial pain regarding LGBTQ issues has reached a critical mass of Catholics, particularly in my North American

---

[7] Ibid., 31.
[8] Hinze, "Ecclesial Impasse," 483.

context. This is not only because the voices of lament have grown louder but also because of a new and surprising willingness of many Catholics to hear voices that previously were shut out of the conversation. Amid the conversations on polarization in the US Catholic Church that prompted these reflections, I have been struck speechless by the fact that Catholic bishops, theologians, scholars, and journalists are actively seeking, despite their different understandings of the morality of same-sex sexual activity, to develop strategies of openness to and dialogue with LGBTQ Catholics and their families. As recently as ten years ago, dialogues like the Notre Dame conference, like that undertaken by the Synod of Bishops, and like the one that continues through the essays in the volume, were quite literally unimaginable. Speaking ecclesial pain out of silence—naming the woundedness of our ecclesial experience—will prove, I believe, to be a hard but necessary form of therapy. The newfound ability of many in our church to speak and to listen about LGBTQ issues and experiences should be a sign of renewed hope in the ability of Christ the Healer to remedy the inflammation of his Body.

6

Polarization and Its Discontents

Holly Taylor Coolman

In the fall of 2013, when Pope Francis announced that he would convoke an extraordinary synod of bishops on the topic of the family, anticipation began to build. It was clear to all observers that families were facing pressures of many kinds, and that the attention of the bishops was well-deserved. It is more than a little poignant, then, two-and-a-half years later, after conversations that occurred around the globe, interviews and essays, a number of major book-length publications, and two major synodal meetings, that one of the clearest outcomes of this initiative is the bitter division it produced. Talking about the family seemed to expose some of the ugliest dynamics in the family of the church itself. In particular, in the United States, it was easy to see the increasingly powerful forces of polarization at work.

It is often assumed that "polarization" is simply another word for "conflict." When pressed to recognize a new and worsening situation of polarization, those who hold to this view note that conflict has been a part of the church's experience from the very beginning. And they are right. Disagreement between individuals, as well as factions and competing schools of thought, have always been present. Even in the first generation, among those following Christ, mutually incompatible positions on important matters appeared. Bishops, councils, creeds, sacred Scripture, and, over time, an identifiable magisterium have sought to resolve these painful divides. But none of it has been easy. The church's unity has never been simple or complete but has always been lived out as a slow, lumbering process.

Polarization, though, is not the same thing as conflict. In fact, I will argue that although polarization can involve conflict, it can also do just the opposite: it can function precisely to prevent necessary and healthy conflict and thus also to prevent the resolution that might ultimately be reached. Here, I share my own reflections on the meaning of polarization in the church today, drawn from my experiences as a citizen, a family member, and a teacher.

As Mary Ellen Konieczny noted in her introduction to this volume, the notion of polarization has its origin in physics. Many of us have seen a simple demonstration that illustrates the basic principle: a bar magnet is lowered into a field of iron shavings, and as a result, the metal shavings cluster in a circle around each pole. Everything within the field of influence of the magnet becomes related to those two opposed poles. There are, of course, two, and only two, orienting poles—and attraction to the one happens precisely in the form of repulsion from the other. Complexity disappears. Varied, intricate interactions fade. One single, simple pattern dominates.

Social situations in which people, organizations, and commitments of various kinds cluster around two poles are described as "polarized," an analogy first seen in political theory. And it is not difficult to see the bipolar pattern currently at work in US politics. Our own political system is organized in relation to two—and only two—parties. As with the magnet, powerful forces require alignment at one end or the other. In the past few decades, especially, the parties have turned inward, demanding ever purer and more total commitment to their respective organizations, and that commitment is often conceived primarily as opposition to the opponents. A Republican who attempts to reach across the aisle will quickly be labeled a "RINO." A Democrat who questions big labor or considers any restriction to abortion access will not be in office for long. Voting records tell the story in their own way. In a study published in 2013, researchers demonstrated that between 1975 and 2012, Republicans and Democrats increasingly diverged in their voting records, while independent voting of any kind has virtually disappeared.[1]

We know only too well what this means in practice. The loss of bipartisanship endeavor is also the loss of certain practices and skills: precise, measured debate; hearing and weighing the concern of the other; considering carefully arguments against one's own position; imaginatively and creatively seeking strategies that break through a perceived impasse. A snowball effect comes into play. More perfect division into two camps means even less opportunity to hear from, much less build relationships with, one's "opponents."

Unfortunately, the US Catholic Church demonstrates the very same tendencies. If the church is a field of iron shavings, then polarization is a bar magnet that reshapes everything in that field according to its own relentless, bipolar force into "conservative" or "liberal." As with the magnetic experiment, this commitment to the extremes involves two, and only two, options, and each is defined precisely by its opposition to the other. The work of polarization is to attempt relentlessly to assign everything that belongs to the church—including people, doctrines, and organizations—to one pole or the other. Theological emphases, political and social commitments, texts and schools, liturgical practices, bishops (including popes), religious orders, even individual lay people: under the sway of polarization, all are divvied up into either the "liberal" or "conservative" camp. So, concern for the unborn is conservative; concern for the undocumented is liberal. A family rosary is conservative;

---

[1] James Moody and Peter J. Mucha, "Portrait of Political Party Polarization," *Network Science* 1, no. 1 (April 15, 2013), http://dx.doi.org/10.1017/nws.2012.3.

a ministry among the homeless is liberal. Chant is conservative; a guitar is liberal. In the case of Catholicism, this is poignant, indeed. Scripture and Tradition, in their many forms, are engaged primarily in order to mine data to support one's own position. In the worst-case scenarios, these gifts of God to the church are weaponized to be used against one another.

In these social situations, furthermore, another dimension of polarization appears. Unlike iron shavings, people and the relationships between them simply do not always line up neatly at one pole or another. Polarization, though, with its simple and unified narrative, offers a temptation: ignore any complexity that stands outside the narrative. Perhaps understandably, our attention and our discourse are unhelpfully dominated by a pattern that is easy to understand and deploy. In politics, it means that not only the media but also the general public fall into speaking much more about the two options of "liberal" and "conservative" than reality warrants. Meanwhile, issues and people that don't neatly fit that narrative fade into the background.

In the case of the two synodal meetings on the family, all this happened with remarkable speed and force. Indeed, before the first synod had even occurred, Cardinal Walter Kasper was invited by Pope Francis to give an opening address and signaled clearly his position: he would press the question of whether Catholics who were divorced and remarried without annulment might, in certain cases, receive Communion. The battle ensued. The synod was covered by Catholic media as if this were the only question at hand. The larger focus of these meetings, and the larger challenges for families, fell from view.

Our imaginations come to be shaped by this way of seeing things. We sometimes come to believe that various ecclesial elements really are the property of one pole or the other. Identification with one pole comes to mean opposition to the other. Those among us who sit most comfortably at one of the two poles face what is perhaps the gravest danger of polarization: we may mistake that pole for the Gospel itself. Meanwhile, as polarization draws all attention to itself, whatever this pattern does not emphasize is overlooked.

We, too, lose the ability to argue with one another well. The dynamics that sort us in this way mitigate against careful, patient conversation. Our engagements become superficial and combative. Good conflict, after all, requires at least two things: that we are present to one another; and that we know that what unites us is greater than what divides us. Both of these necessary conditions are undermined by polarization. So, that vicious circle appears: each pole only hardens further and further in antipathy to the other, and mutual opposition becomes a self-perpetuating phenomenon.

My own experience with marriage and family suggests a similar problem. In our vocation as parents, what my husband and I feel most often is our need for an active and engaged local parish community, a larger family in which our own nuclear family can not only gather for worship but also support others and be supported in the everyday work of loving God and others. In a context where people are often separated from extended family, or where extended family are not always practicing the faith, we know we are not alone in that. At least one survey confirms that we are not. In an informal survey taken just before the Synod on the Family, respondents—including parents, godparents, and church leaders—indicated that the single most important message they sought from the church was "You are welcome here." A close second was "How can the church help you / your family live out your faith in the world?" Every other possible response lagged far, far beyond.[2] At least in the United States, then, it would seem that building up parishes as vibrant places for families as well as single people to engage, might be treated as singularly important. In

---

[2] "What Do Parents Want to Hear from the Church? A Survey Analysis Conducted by the Strong Catholic Families National Initiative," http://www .strongcatholicfamilies.org/docs/whatParentsWanttoHearfromChurch-Final .pdf.

recent conversations about family, we might have expected that it would receive significant time and attention. How was it, then, that the question of Communion for divorced-and-remarried Catholics and the ensuing, polarized battle over this question dominated so completely?

Conversations with students in the classroom also demonstrate for me the shortcomings of polarization. In some ways, my students seem "liberal." They come to our conversations about marriage family with concerns about the church's "conservative" leanings. The church teaches that sex is sinful, they believe, and there is a crazy rule about birth control. In other ways, they seem "conservative." They revere marriage. On the subject of marital fidelity, they leave absolutely no room for any lapse, and they tend also to be vehemently opposed to divorce. Many say that it would be far better never to marry than it is to end a marriage in divorce.

As we go on to discuss a sacramental account of marriage more fully, their responses are even harder to label. The most common response is one of genuine curiosity, even intrigue. Most of my students are Catholic. Many arrive at the Catholic college where I teach having just completed thirteen years of Catholic education. Nevertheless, some of the basic elements of Catholic marriage are surprising to them. When I explain that the church teaches not that one should not end a sacramental marriage, but that one cannot end a sacramental marriage, they are often struck by the very notion of a permanent vow. ("You're saying that you can choose something, and then you don't have any way to un-choose it?") In the most recent instance, one young woman found curious the idea that a marriage vow could be interrupted by death. ("Why would that be?" she asked.) By the time we get to more controversial topics, they have usually begun to move past any kneejerk response.

I walk away with my own set of concerns. These wonderful, bright students, many of whom belong to the church and some of whom even claim their Catholic identity enthusiastically, seem to know little of what the Catholic tradition offers. They see marriage as difficult and demanding. Even those who see marriage in their future often insist it would not fit into their plan "anytime soon." For many, it simply looks like an enormous leap, and one they cannot picture themselves making.

I believe that polarization has failed them. They don't fit neatly into categories of "liberal" and "conservative"—or even into a spectrum construed as a straight line between the two. The questions that they do have are ones that are lost in the pitched battle between opposing camps. At the same time, as I interact with them, it seems to me that providing them with the resources they need in approaching marriage and family is an important and urgent ecclesial task. It should surely appear very high on any list of priorities. Why, then, was it not central in our communal conversations about family?

Overall, therefore, we face two great challenges. Polarization has divided us up and would divide us further. It shrinks our imaginations to fit its own pattern, which although elegant in its simplicity, fails radically to capture the church as it is or the church as it is called to be. It erases complexity, and it transforms meaningful conflict into sneering dismissal.

At the same time, however, even where polarization has not fully succeeded, we sometimes speak and act as if it has. The American Catholic Church is not, in fact, divided up perfectly according to polarization's magnetic pull. The two options of "liberal" and "conservative" do not make sense of many people's experience, and so crucially important questions and concerns are simply overlooked. It is important to say with regard to individual people that there are certainly some Catholics who feel fully at home at one of these two poles. They have their own challenge: in that case, there is always the possibility that commitment to the Catholic faith can shrivel to being nothing more than commitment to that pole.

The challenges are serious. The question is what can be done to respond to them, and that will require a much larger conversation to answer. Whatever shape that conversation takes, however, it is clear: we can do better.

Part 3

Assessing the Problem

7

Left/Right Polarization as Culture Wars Captivity

One Scholar's Journey and Analysis

David P. Gushee

My Sojourn

The left/right polarization so ubiquitous in American politics and culture affects all religious traditions in our country, including the Catholicism in which I was raised in the late 1960s (and to which I have returned in recent years), the Southern Baptist faith to which I converted as a teenager in the 1970s, the mainline Protestant context in which I undertook my doctorate in the 1980s, and the evangelicalism with which I began to identify in the 1990s. The same holds for the three schools (all of them Baptist) at which I have been a full-time professor and the two major religion-scholar associations in which I have participated as an academician.

The religious communities I just mentioned are quite distinctive branches of American Christianity. One would immediately be able to tell the differences between them on a Sunday morning in worship or at chapel in any of their respective universities or seminaries. And my experiences in each have been very different—with one exception. All have been marked by the evidences of left/right polarization.

Those evidences have been visible both in conflict and in consensus. Conflict has been ubiquitous and painful when

left-leaning and right-leaning participants within these traditions have clashed. I have lived through a number of these
clashes. Consensus, far less frequent, has been visible when
the ideological primacy of one side has triumphed so completely that adherents of the other side have evacuated the
premises. The all-left or all-right echo chamber thus created
is then itself striking evidence of polarization.

To spell out my own journey in a bit more detail: I was raised
in post–Vatican II Catholicism in Vienna, Virginia. St. Mark's
parish, at the time, leaned left. In 1978, when I was sixteen, I
stumbled into Providence Baptist Church in Tyson's Corner, Virginia, and became a born-again convert. (I often have attributed
my openness to a Southern Baptist conversion as a teenager to
the weak-porridge Catholicism on offer at St. Mark's parish.)
Though there was some diversity in the congregation, on the
whole this Southern Baptist congregation leaned strongly right.

After attending a slightly left-leaning Southern Baptist Theological Seminary for my ministry degree, I went to the mainline
Protestant Union Theological Seminary in New York for my
ethics doctorate. There, the range of acceptable opinion ran
from liberal to radical. The rest of us stayed pretty quiet.

I took my first job in 1990 with the Canadian evangelical Ron
Sider, who leaned left on most issues but right on sexual ethics.
In 1993 I returned to Louisville to teach at Southern Seminary,
which had been subjected to an intentional conservative take-
over and was just about to swing hard-right, throwing many
casualties overboard. I moved after three years to Union University in West Tennessee, which was still Southern Baptist and
also leaned right, though it was under more irenic leadership.

In 2007, I moved to left-leaning Mercer University here in
Georgia. At the time, I still called myself a Baptist and an evangelical but tried to occupy a *centrist* space in both camps.[1] In
the decade since coming to Mercer, I have watched that space

---

[1] See Gushee, *The Future of Faith in American Politics* (Waco, TX: Baylor,
2008).

shrink, and now, most often, I am identified (even identify myself) as a progressive Baptist and evangelical—except by those to my right, who often wish to label me as post-Baptist, post-evangelical, maybe post-God.

Another wrinkle: my wife Jeanie converted to Catholicism some fifteen years ago. A few years ago, here in Atlanta, I worked through a process with our local Catholic parish in order to return as a full communicant—without abandoning my Baptist job or congregation. So I am biconfessional. Our local parish, Holy Cross Catholic Church, seems pretty apolitical, which is refreshing. I experience right-wing Catholicism, however, when I visit my father and sister in Front Royal, Virginia, home of Christendom College and a very, very conservative local parish, St. John the Baptist.

What I Mean By "Left" and "Right"

One characteristic of our polarized times is that the polarization is increasingly comprehensive. It as if two all-powerful magnets, one to our "left" and the other to our "right," eventually grab most Americans and pull us in one direction or the other. Hardly anyone seems exempt, and hardly any aspect of any individual seems exempt.

One way to break this down might be to identify the polarization as having political, cultural, and religious dimensions. Those on the left are on the left *politically,* identifying as progressive or liberal on all different kinds of policy issues and voting Democratic (or to the Bernie Sanders-left-of-Democratic). They are on the left *culturally*, by which I mean supporting cultural change rather than stasis, with a focus on the inclusion of more and more previously marginalized groups and a breaking of white male hegemony. And they are on the left *religiously*, which sometimes means holding loosely or abandoning some traditional doctrinal or ethical positions and almost always means identifying with a version of Christianity and with deceased or current Christian leaders that lean left as they do. The obverse would hold true for those on the right.

I offer a Baptist example. The (white) Baptist left, at least in the South, identifies as progressive or liberal and overwhelmingly votes Democratic. They favor full equality for women in the churches and generally embrace the social change and social justice agenda of the left. They sometimes hold loosely to some traditional doctrinal or ethical positions. They almost always identify with Baptist leaders like Social Gospel leader Walter Rauschenbusch, civil rights icon Martin Luther King, Jr., and former president Jimmy Carter.

The Baptist right, on the other hand, identifies as politically conservative and overwhelmingly votes Republican. They generally do not support women's ordination and reject most or all of the social change and social justice agenda of the left. (Race makes for an interesting, arguable, exception.) They hold tightly to pretty much all traditional doctrinal and ethical positions. They identify with Baptist leaders like theologian Carl F. H. Henry, former Nixon aide and born-again activist Chuck Colson, and former Arkansas governor Mike Huckabee.

Southern Baptists fought a vicious internal war between 1979 and 1991, leading to the fragmentation of our community into three different denominations or fellowships. The Southern Baptist Convention, which retained most white, southern, Baptist congregations and members after the fight was over, came under the control of a very conservative movement and has since remained very conservative. (There's your Baptist right.) Ex-Southern Baptist liberals formed the Alliance of Baptists. (There's your Baptist left.) A middle group, the Cooperative Baptist Fellowship, contains congregations and individuals who lean left, center, and right. Those churches are generally struggling, and fear of the eruption of left/right divisions and the splintering of this relatively small fellowship cripples the young Christian quasi denomination.

It is precisely the comprehensiveness of the polarization that is so striking. There is no intrinsic reason why just about every aspect of the life of a religious person or group should fly to the left or the right as if by magnetic attraction. Neither in the history of any of the groups I have mentioned, nor in the current life of the international Baptist, Catholic, or evangelical family, does left/right polarization work itself out quite so comprehensively. This appears to be a distinctively US phenomenon, at least to a very large extent, and a distinctively contemporary one.

So what exactly happened that got us to this point?

Culture War Theories

The first major analysis of the situation we are still facing in America was offered by sociologist James Davison Hunter in his groundbreaking 1991 book *Culture Wars: The Struggle to Define America*.[2] Hunter described the situation as a worldview clash between groups he called "orthodox" and "progressive" (equivalent to my "right" and "left"). These groups, especially as embodied by their activists, viscerally differ over "our most fundamental and cherished assumptions about how to order our lives" individually and in society.[3] These are "competing moral visions" so distinct as to create "polarizing impulses or tendencies" throughout American culture, even though, said Hunter twenty-five years ago, "[M]ost Americans occupy a vast middle ground."[4] (One wonders whether he would still make that claim today.)

According to Hunter, competing worldviews, mainly competing understandings of the source and nature of moral truth, lie at the heart of the culture wars. These differences lead to different normative moral beliefs about a wide range of particular issues. They also tend to produce different postures toward culture as well as different "political dispositions." Thus on the one side are cultural "conservatives" and "moral

---

[2] *Culture Wars: The Struggle to Define America* (New York: Basic Books, 1991).

[3] Ibid., 42.

[4] Ibid., 43.

traditionalists," while on the other side are cultural and moral "progressives" or "liberals."

At the time Hunter wrote his book, the alignment of the platforms and agendas of our two major political parties with these two sides of the culture wars had not progressed nearly as far as it has today. Though there are certainly exceptions, such as pro-life Democrats and pro-gay Republicans, today the Democrats generally align with the culture wars "left" and the Republicans with the culture wars "right." Hunter noted the beginnings of this trend in his book and asked the trenchant question "who is using whom?" Are the culture warriors using the politicians or the politicians using the culture warriors? By now, it is sometimes hard to tell the difference.

A more politically focused analysis with a somewhat longer time frame has been offered by Rick Perlstein in his trilogy of recent books on the rise of modern political conservatism. *Before the Storm* focuses on 1964 Republican presidential nominee Barry Goldwater and the circumstances preceding and surrounding his run.[5] *Nixonland* describes the career of the inimitable Richard Nixon but along the way offers a stunning description of America in the turbulent 1960s.[6] Similarly, *The Invisible Bridge* tells the story of the rise of Ronald Reagan to the presidency against the backdrop of the events of the 1970s.[7]

Together, these hefty tomes weigh in at 2400 pages, so there is far too much to summarize here. Let me offer the following synthesis.

The left/right polarization that we know so well is inextricable from the birth of the modern conservative movement in the 1950s. That movement began with two major pillars: staunch anti-Communism in the context of the Cold War, often accompanied by support for a hawkish policy in relating to the nuclear-armed USSR, and small-government economic

---

[5] Rick Perlstein, *Before the Storm* (New York: Nation Books, 2001).

[6] Rick Perlstein, *Nixonland* (New York: Scribner, 2008).

[7] Rick Perlstein, *The Invisible Bridge* (New York: Simon & Schuster, 2014).

libertarianism birthed in reaction to the policies of Franklin Roosevelt's New Deal.

The developments of the 1960s added a third major pillar: cultural conservatism. This cultural conservatism erupted in reaction to the sexual revolution, the gay rights movement, the women's movement, the drug culture, the wild campus protests, the widespread opposition to the Vietnam War, and, of course, racial integration and the civil rights movement. After 1973, the national decriminalization of abortion became a major new element on this list, to which other items were constantly added as other culture war battlegrounds emerged.

Barry Goldwater, Richard Nixon, and, most effectively, Ronald Reagan, created a new Republican coalition and a new version of conservatism that combined all three of these pillars: staunch anti-Communism (together with hawkish foreign policy and American exceptionalism, unilateralism, and national pride), small-government/antitax/pro-business economics, and moral traditionalism on issues such as sex, drugs, family, and abortion. On race, the somewhat more veiled white conservative line was advanced through a variety of proxies such as opposition to affirmative action and to enforced school busing for racial integration.

Democrats, on the other hand, often (though not always) offered a less hawkish, softer foreign policy line, while always offering a diametrically opposed set of economic policies, support for racial integration, and "minority uplift" efforts (after the decline of the Southern Democrats), and a fairly consistent moral progressivism on sex, family, and abortion, if not drugs.

The "culture wars" have often been understood to include only the last element of this triad, but in broader perspective, the pulling together of foreign and military policy, economic policy, and cultural issues defines the comprehensive political, moral, cultural, and even religious polarization that we face today. Look at the Democratic and Republican Party platforms of any election year and they will generally fall in with these broad lines of demarcation, to which other issues could be added today such as immigration, Israel/Palestine, the Common Core, and so much more.

The most recent major book on the subject, *A War for the Soul of America*, is by historian Andrew Hartman.[8] Hartman starts his story at a different place as he locates the origins of the culture wars in the New Left of the 1960s, with all of the challenges to traditional values already outlined.

Hartman then focuses his attention on a kind of two-stage conservative pushback. First came the neoconservatives, mainly Jews and Catholics, such as Norman Podhoretz and Daniel Patrick Moynihan. In the very early 1970s, they attacked the agenda of the New Left, especially on race, gender, and education. Later in the 1970s, the Protestant fundamentalists and evangelicals joined the neocons in an uneasy coalition, bringing their characteristic concerns with such issues as abortion. This alignment has been consistently opposed by heirs to the New Left; this conflict has defined our era, though Hartman suggests that the culture wars pretty much had wound down by the late 1990s.

Weariness and Hope

When I began my career, I had hope that the culture wars would eventually run their course, and I could enjoy at least some years in a different kind of cultural, political, and religious context. Alas, here in 2016 I am quite sure that this is not the case—and will not be the case for the decade or so that I plan to continue pursuing this wearying work in Christian social ethics.

Our politics have hardened into semipermanent culture war categories. Large parts of our media have joined the polarization. Social media only makes it worse. And many religious communities have simply splintered, formally or informally, along left/right lines.

---

[8] Andrew Hartman, *A War for the Soul of America* (Chicago: The University of Chicago Press, 2015).

The Catholic organizers of the Notre Dame conference on polarization and of this conference volume certainly hope to contribute to a culture, or at least a church, that can get beyond such polarization. It is indeed a worthy goal, for no Christian ought to see our capitulation to a relatively recent, very American, totally contingent polarization as anything other than a defeat for Christian integrity and unity.

Scanning the entire Christian landscape, I find in the Roman Catholic Church one of my only sources of hope. Catholicism has a long historical memory, so it knows better than to identify current circumstances with eternal truths. It is international, so it has resources for getting beyond parochially American categories and patterns. It has resources in Catholic theology and ethics that challenge simple left/right binaries. And it appears impervious to a full-blown institutional left/right split as might happen with a Protestant congregation or denomination.

This means that those American Catholics leaning left, leaning right, and leaning center must continue to relate to each other, as sisters and brothers in Christ, like it or not. As they do, they have the broader resources of the Catholic tradition available to point them to a path of Christian integrity and unity.

8

The Art of Accompaniment

Amy Uelmen

At work, at school, in our families, parishes, and communities, we seem to be increasingly barraged by signs of deep disagreement and the sense that we are talking past rather than with each other. This leaves many with the sense that it might be close to impossible to understand one another across these cultural, social, religious, and political differences.

When profound disagreements surface, some who strongly identify with a religious tradition experience a profound tension between, on the one hand, the desire to maintain both the principles they hold and a belief that these principles should inform a vision of what is good for our communities and, on the other hand, the desire to be part of the work of building open, loving, trusting relationships.

These questions become even more complex when we consider the dynamic of how teenagers and young adults are approaching these tensions. Recent research indicates that individuals in the Millennial generation, those born in the early 1980s to about 2000, have a heightened sensitivity to the value of relationships. For example, when asked to identify "one of the most important things in their lives," 52 percent responded being a good parent; 30 percent, having a successful marriage; 21 percent, helping others in need; and only 15 percent having a high paying career.[1] While there are obvious upsides to this focus, fragilities emerge when this sensitivity takes the form of excessive attention to social appearances. As a result, many young adults find it difficult to articulate what is important to them. They also struggle mightily with a strong aversion to ever judging any aspect of other people's choices or identity.

When cultural and religious polarization is combined with these deep aversions to ever judging any aspect of other people's choices or identity, the brew can be toxic for those who hope to create spaces for honest conversation about commitment for the good in a variety of social, cultural, and educational environments. What kind of frame might help us to move through and beyond these challenges? This essay addresses this question.

In the encyclical *Mater et Magistra* (On Christianity and Social Progress), Pope John XXIII articulated the now-classic method for reflection in Catholic Social Thought: "see, judge, act" (MM 236).[2] Let's face squarely some of the cultural challenges that this model seems to present at this point in our history. First, it can be difficult to *see*, or to create a basis for communication about what one sees, when we have a hard time agreeing that any one lens has the correct vision. *Judge*: I do not think for a second that in this context, the word "judge" was intended to mean "be judgmental." Nonetheless, it can be hard to get around how this word seems to trigger connection with what has become our society's "cardinal sin"—to judge another person. Finally, *act*, without further refinement, is easily associated with the less than healthy side of take-charge

---

[1] Pew Research Center, *Millennials: A Portrait of Generation Next*, http://pewresearch.org/millennials/. See generally Morley Winograd and Michael D. Hais, *Millennial Momentum: How a New Generation Is Remaking America* (New Brunswick, NJ: Rutgers University Press, 2011).

[2] John XXIII, *Mater et Magistra* (On Christianity and Social Progress), May 15, 1961, http://w2.vatican.va/content/john-xxiii/en/encyclicals/documents /hf_j-xxiii_enc_15051961_mater.html. Hereafter MM.

or take-control activism that can detract from the respect that more relational and reciprocal approaches might convey.

Of course, each of these keywords, and the profound values they continue to represent, could be retrieved and reframed based on what we have learned over the course of world and church history since the Second Vatican Council. That would be one strategy. Another strategy is to find new keywords and phrases. One candidate for a new formulation can be found in the key phrases of the October 2014 *Interim Report on the Pastoral Challenges of the Family*: (1) listen; (2) look to the face of Christ; (3) face the situation. How might these concepts enrich our frame for analyzing a religious contribution to social commitment?

First, *listen*. To me, this suggests a need to hear and take in the voices and stories of others. Listening conveys a sense of receptivity. Of course, like "seeing," "hearing" is not immune from the risk of filtering the reality of the other according to one's own categories or criteria. But what I like about the word "listen" is that it tends to invite an interior quiet in order to create a space to receive the reality of the other.

Second, *look to the face of Christ*. I believe this can both simplify and complicate the criteria for "judgment." What might it mean to say that to "judge" or evaluate a situation is completely wrapped up in the movement of "looking to Christ"? In this, we may catch a glimpse of the embrace between love and truth and the kiss of justice and peace.

Third, *face the situation*. This might be more open textured than *act*. It could convey a stance, a sense of engaging the reality, but without specifying the exact form of engagement. Sometimes the best way to build a communal response to a particular challenge is to leave space for it to percolate and to sustain the process of reflection from within, from underneath— so that protagonists from within a given community can let their own proposals mature as they discern what to do.

How might this framework inform a pastoral action plan against the backdrop of the questions and tensions discussed above, with a particular eye to young adults? My experience with this group is primarily in two contexts: first, teaching law school seminars at the intersection of religious values and professional life; and second, accompanying young adults who desire to grow in the Focolare spirituality of unity. In both contexts, I have been struck by how their sense of disorientation and fear of being judgmental can damage their sense of integrity and paralyze the decision-making process. The sections below explore how each of these keywords, also illuminated by Pope Francis's insights in the apostolic exhortation *Evangelii Gaudium* (On the Proclamation of the Gospel in Today's World) may serve as a guide and a resource for healing this sense of fragmentation.[3]

Listening: Presence and Privacy

In my experience, when people feel that you are able to receive their reality—to understand their experience and their concerns—and that the insights you share are grounded in this receptivity rather than a preconceived agenda, it is rare that they feel judged. In this context, they may also begin to develop pretty good instincts for what it means not to be judgmental in how they consider others. How might we work to create this kind of communicative space with and among young adults?

I think it is hard to overestimate just how pervasive is Millennials' sense of always being "on," of performing before some kind of camera or internet broadcast, hoping to satisfy social expectations and definitions of happiness and success. As Pope Francis describes: "In the prevailing culture, priority is given to the outward, the immediate, the visible, the quick,

---

[3] Francis, Apostolic Exhortation *Evangelii Gaudium* (On the Proclamation of the Gospel in Today's World), November 24, 2013, https://w2.vatican.va /content/francesco/en/apost_exhortations/documents/papa-francesco _esortazione-ap_20131124_evangelii-gaudium.html. Hereafter EG.

the superficial and the provisional. What is real gives way to appearances" (EG 62).

These dynamics make it especially difficult to discern in what people say and do what is important and meaningful, what is banal, and what is just stupid. Further, the pace and reactive nature of the media can detract from the reflective space people need to fully work out what they think. In contrast to relationships mediated "by screens and systems which can be turned on and off on command," Pope Francis recalls the Gospel challenge "to run the risk of a face-to-face encounter with others, with their physical presence which challenges us" (EG 88).[4]

In an overly wired culture, a commitment to listen will often invoke two increasingly rare qualities: presence and privacy. Full presence and undivided attention can be conveyed in numerous ways—for example, making the time and space for an in-person meeting and switching off all forms of media connection and other distractions. When possible, I even put my watch out of my sight. For students, personalized feedback on their written submissions and a class discussion agenda formed on the basis of their observations and priorities can help to convey a continuous sense that not only am I paying close attention to what they say but also that I am taking it seriously as the driver for our class discussion.

In a polarized culture, especially when the conversation involves working through experience, opinions, or insights on difficult personal issues such as abortion or sexual identity, it

---

[4] I believe this statement could also be read as a kind of papal endorsement of a policy to ban laptops in certain circumstances. At least in a seminar, laptop screens are a physical barrier to the body language that can help us fully receive what the other is saying. And when even one person in the room is shopping, checking e-mail, or playing games, I have found that it can be very difficult to generate the kind of trust we need to talk about questions that really matter to people. I sense that at least some students agree and are relieved when laptops are removed from the learning environment. As one of my students put it: "This semester I am fortunate enough to be in two classes that ban laptops."

can also be helpful to create a certain zone of privacy. Unplugging from the tendency to post ideas to the world on social media can help to provide a space in which young adults are able to test out how to express themselves without getting tied in knots over the extent to which their tentative efforts might be perceived as a judgment of others. For certain topics, some people may also need an initial steam valve or a space outside of the pressure-cooker of a more public discussion in order to work through dimensions of anger, pain, or confusion. Having an initial sounding board that is private can help to build trust and often leads to the capacity to be more discerning in framing positions for more public conversations.

What is the impact of this focused presence and attention to the need for privacy? In the past few years of working with Millennials, I have been fascinated by how a kind of "pay it forward" dynamic emerges in which they tend to turn with open ears and hearts to their cohorts. For many, these relationships constitute a healthy social context in which they can detoxify from exhausting social posturing and competition that can so damage the processes of discerning and articulating one's own commitments and building sincere relationships of trust with others.

Three Ways to "Look to the Face of Christ"

The second key phrase in the synod document is "Look to the Face of Christ." For those who are worried about judging or being judged, isn't this kind of an odd move? Wouldn't the particularity of delving into such a specific source or orientation and identity exacerbate rather than heal those polarizing divides? I have seen how this move to specificity produces exactly the opposite effect. In other words, the deeper one's sense of being grounded in profound values and commitments—which, in non-Christian contexts, can be instead the move to a transcendent point of reference, or a moral anchor—the more one can find a sure foundation to engage others who may think differently.

One key to unlocking this connection is to see that the process of finding my own moral anchor—how I understand my own values, and how I explain them to the people closest to me—can be *distinguished* from the project of learning how to talk about my values in a pluralistic professional or social setting. They may require different conceptual equipment and different linguistic tools, but *both* can be acts of love.

In my conversations with young adults, I often reach for images. With a student who was frequently looking around the room before saying anything, testing the waters before committing to an idea, we imagined a revamped version of that gimmicky Staples button to indicate the ease of ordering from the store ("that was easy") to say instead, "Don't worry." I challenged: "Whenever you are starting to look around, press that button, and then reach within, to try to give something from the depths of yourself to your colleagues. Don't worry whether what you say will be completely understood—focus instead on the sense of freedom that emerges as you offer your gift." Within just a few weeks of this practice, this student had blossomed with a beautiful sense of openness and trust.

With others, we have worked with a plastic image of Ignatian discernment: a sifter that when placed in front of God at the end of the day is able to distinguish sand, which represents the play to appearances, from the nuggets of gold that indicate a sense of integrity and a capacity to build sincere relationships. With still others, the image has been from Jeremiah and the Psalms, contrasting the bush in the desert with the tree planted near running water that bears fruit in due season, so as to focus on those underground roots that no one sees and to be peaceful with the time lag in seeing results. Look within, make contact with the presence of God within—however you name that presence—and locate it as a precious guide for your life. That is the first way to "look to the face of Christ."

The deeper people are able to put down these roots, the more they grow in the capacity to turn toward their colleagues to build relationships of trust. This is a second way to look to the face of Christ. Pope Francis is eloquent on how this connection can help to build strong relationships of trust: "[T]o learn how to encounter others with the right attitude, which is to accept and esteem them as companions along the way, without interior resistance. Better yet, it means learning to find Jesus in the faces of others, in their voices, in their pleas" (EG 91). And this in turn also generates the capacity to keep an open heart and mind even in an encounter with uncomfortable or grating differences: "It is a fraternal love capable of seeing the sacred grandeur of our neighbor, of finding God in every human being, of tolerating the nuisances of life in common by clinging to the love of God, of opening the heart to divine love and seeking the happiness of others just as their heavenly Father does" (EG 92).

Finally, when I think of looking to the face of Christ as a source of orientation, the greatest resource for me is the image of (or better, the relationship with) Jesus on the cross, the God who cried, "Why have you forsaken me?" (Mark 15:34; cf. Matt 27:46). The pressure that young adults feel to keep a tight sense of control over all of the elements of their lives seems to leave very little space for recognizing and processing the reality of suffering—illness, death, fears about violence in the world, or even more daily and mundane disappointments and failures. But in many ways, the capacity to look to this face of Christ can provide a deep source of perspective, hope, and deep connection with others.

As Pope Francis challenged: "Jesus wants us to touch human misery, to touch the suffering flesh of others . . . [to] enter into the reality of other people's lives and know the power of tenderness. Whenever we do so, our lives become wonderfully complicated and we experience intensely what it is to be a people, to be part of a people" (EG 270). When I recognize that at the heart of so many of polarizing cultural debates is a person, or persons, who are feeling lacerated, disoriented, and alone, it is good to sit with the questions: When I think about the persons who are suffering in the midst of these "issues," is it with all of the love that I hope to have for a wounded Jesus on the cross? Is my perspective grounded in an effort to enter and live inside those wounds?

"Face the Situation" as a Frame for Discernment

What I like about the "face the situation" frame is how it seems to leave room for responsive discernment regarding what to do in a given situation. Immediate action may be appropriate, or it may not. In some circumstances, it might be best to let responsive resolutions percolate through various layers of involvement and participation in order to foster broader ownership over a particular response. Of course, the word "act" would not necessarily preclude this kind of deliberation. But "face the situation" holds the potential for surfacing and highlighting a more reflective and deliberative quality.

One problem, of course, is that all of this deliberative space in discussions about what to do can be overwhelmed by deep and seemingly irresolvable conflict. For example, in some discussions about the polarizing questions of our day, such as abortion, same-sex marriage, or euthanasia, it can quickly become evident that the working definitions of "harm" within different philosophical systems may be so *vastly* different that it is difficult to imagine how engagement between conversation partners may be anything other than "ships passing in the night." Moreover, some young adults are at the beginning of their efforts to fine-tune their social, cultural, rhetorical, and dialogue skills, which means that they may not know how to wade into a discussion of conflict over these charged issues.

In discussions with very pluralistic groups, a comparative approach may help to provide a frame for discussion in which various systems of thought are recognized in their integrity, with their own history, contours, and claims. The project may be understood as not focused on getting anyone to necessarily change their perspective but rather on working to *understand* the claims and to offer narratives that can help humanize the reasons that may lie behind conflicting claims.

For conversations in which the Catholic intellectual tradition is a point of reference, the November 2002 *Doctrinal Note* from the Congregation for the Doctrine of the Faith includes a helpful distinction between clarity on values or principles and the permissible variety within possible strategies and avenues for concrete political action. It is important to note that every issue—including those that involve "intrinsic evils"—requires some deliberation and practical analysis on the question about exactly what to do. It is also helpful to note when this, rather than a clash of principles, is the source of disagreement. For example, on the question of abortion, we need the political process to work through what to do about it, how to reduce it, and how every person, including the unborn, can be treated with dignity and respect. Because it is not immediately clear how to answer these questions, differences of opinion are legitimate, appropriate, and perhaps even helpful.

For those who hope to be simultaneously rooted in church tradition and teaching and open to the world's sufferings and questions, how much room is there for discussion about exactly what to do? A wide horizon for engagement opens when we recognize that discussions are *not* only about identifying principles and values but also about the human drama, the challenge, and the suffering people experience in trying to live according to these values, as well as how to meet their particular needs with loving compassion. This points back to the importance of listening: in order to receive the stories and the lives of others, to take on their burdens, and in many circumstances, to recognize in these circumstances the face of Jesus on the cross.

This framework does not, of course, guarantee that there will not be clashes among perspectives or hurt feelings. Many who work with young adults of this generation are focused on creating a safe rhetorical space for them to express themselves. Me too. But I think we need to look further—or we may miss opportunities to help create safer spaces in society. What happens when contrasting views about what to do get squished down or banished from conversation in the various venues of our common life? Where do they go? Often they simply fester and the infection feeds further polarization in our society—especially as people walk away from conversations without the tools or skills that could help them constructively engage profound difference.

So what to do when people are rough—even very rough— around the edges? When intentions are not bad, how can we open a conversation about the pain that is caused—in a way that leads to learning for the future? I recently faced an incident in which I realized that someone from the vast religious majority in the room had really hurt one of the few people in a religious minority, and very few of the others in the conversation were sensitive enough to pick up on the nuance. Talking with the person who was hurt, we discerned together how to work with the fact that each of us is a work in progress—none of us really know yet (or at least not fully) how to carry our convictions, identity, and commitments into a pluralistic, and in this case, professional, environment.

"Facing the situation" together helped to generate a non-threatening communication tool to help raise awareness of the need for a leap in empathy, sensitivity, complexity, and diversity of perspectives. We called it the "SOS" card, an acronym for "step into the other side." The core ideas we agreed on for using the card were as follows:

- You can raise the SOS card regardless of whether your concern emerges from your own personal identity or from an empathetic concern about what others might be feeling.
- Concerns can cover a vast range of questions and concerns, including political stances or identities (race, ethnicity, class, religion, gender, sexual orientation, etc.).
- We agree to receive the SOS signal not as an accusation or a threat but as helpful suggestion to bring into our conversations additional layers of complexity.

- We agree to give priority to these flags in the timing of our conversations, so as to benefit in real time from these suggestions for further attentiveness.

Because the card was introduced at a point at which significant trust had already developed, it was never abused, and it helped to sensitize us as a group to a range of issues, including some that I had not even imagined. By giving each other a kind of x-ray of our interior struggles—trusting that this would be received neither as a judgment of others nor in an attitude of judgment by others—we were able to identify and work through these challenges together.

Conclusion

What makes these key concepts explored powerful and illuminating, not only for journeying together with young adults but also for nurturing any kind of relationship? The art of listening, of fully receiving the other, can sustain a life-giving sense of contact with the face of Christ, which can, in turn, illuminate the process of discernment in a given circumstance. In this dynamic, love of God and love of neighbor are not only linked but also held together in a mutually reinforcing relationship.[5] Using an image which is frequently invoked for the radical otherness of God—the burning bush—Pope Francis describes the "art of accompaniment" as learning how to "remove our sandals before the sacred ground of the other (cf. *Ex* 3:5)" (EG 169).

---

[5] See Chiara Lubich, *Essential Writings* (New York: New City Press, 2007), 65. "Our inner life is fed by our outer life. The more I enter into the soul of my brother or sister, the more I enter into God within me. The more I enter into God within me, the more I enter into my brother or sister. God—myself—my brother or sister: it is all one world, all one kingdom." See also Amelia J. Uelmen, "*Caritas in Veritate* and Chiara Lubich: Human Development from the Vantage Point of Unity," *Theological Studies* 71 (2010): 29–45, here 35–36.

And this dynamic can, in turn, evoke a powerful sense of gratitude, because contact with our neighbor actually fosters and reinforces what we most desire: deeper union with God. As Pope Francis explains:

> When we live out a spirituality of drawing nearer to others and seeking their welfare, our hearts are opened wide to the Lord's greatest and most beautiful gifts. Whenever we encounter another person in love, we learn something new about God. Whenever our eyes are opened to acknowledge the other, we grow in the light of faith and knowledge of God. (EG 272)

This is the light that can then inform the kind of respectful closeness that can help to heal, liberate, and encourage positive growth.

9

When Discourse Breaks Down

Race and Aesthetic Solidarity in the US Catholic Church

Nichole M. Flores

Race and Polarization: A Sign of the Times

Racism is America's original sin, serving as the backdrop for the abuse, exploitation, and marginalization of dark-skinned bodies in every era of our nation's history.[1] Attending to the signs of the times, we discern a disturbing pattern emerging in our society: the frequent and violent deaths of unarmed black men, women, and children at the hands of law enforcement officers. Michael Brown, Eric Garner, Tamir Rice. This litany resonates in our national memory. We reel at the destruction of human life.

Racial justice is often excluded from the list of culture war issues causing deep divisions in the Catholic Church. Yet polarization on issues of racial justice is evident in competing understandings of how to address racial issues in the twenty-first century. Some of us argue that talking about racism actually perpetuates these destructive divisions. Racism is a set

---

[1] See M. Shawn Copeland, "Revisiting Racism," *America* magazine 211, no. 1 (July 7–14, 2014), http://americamagazine.org/issue/revisiting-racism.

of personal actions. If everyone stops engaging in these sinful actions, then society will move past its racism. In this view, the best response to racism is to bury it deep in our historical memory and try to do better as we move forward. Others, however, claim that silence on racial issues is the source of this enduring conflict. Racism is latent in human hearts and social structures; eradicating it thus requires confronting painful histories. Facing dangerous memories—dreadful legacies of slavery, lynching, segregation, and marginalization—is a crucial step to pursuing racial justice. The disagreement is thus an insidious source of division among US Catholics in the twenty-first century.

Several black Catholic theologians have argued that the former strategy has led to the omission of injustices committed against dark-skinned bodies from Catholic Social Teaching.[2] As M. Shawn Copeland explains, "Racism shapes our ideas, attitudes, and dispositions; directs our cultural norms, rules, and expectations; guides our linguistic, literary, artistic, media representations and practices."[3] Racism runs deep, infecting human hearts and damaging the common good. This analysis, they claim, illustrates a painful truth about Catholicism and racism: silence won't work. Christian discipleship necessitates difficult conversations about racism in order to reveal its dangers and cast it out of our church and society.

I concur that racism is a dangerous moral evil that must be confronted by the Body of Christ. But how do we have this difficult conversation across cultural, political, and theological differences? Instead of asking *whether* we should talk

---

[2] See Bryan Massingale, "The Systematic Erasure of the Black/Dark-Skinned Body in Catholic Ethics," in *Catholic Theological Ethics, Past, Present, and Future: The Trento Conference*, ed. James F. Keenan (Maryknoll, NY: Orbis Books, 2011).

[3] M. Shawn Copeland, "Overcoming Christianity's Lingering Complicity," *Syndicate Theology*, July 20, 2015, https://syndicatetheology.com /commentary/overcoming-christianitys-lingering-complicity/.

about race, this essay asks *how* we can do so constructively amid our immensely diverse Catholic Church and public life. Specifically, how should we approach racial conversations in plural contexts when discourse breaks down? I argue that conversations about racial equality and justice can benefit from *aesthetic solidarity*, which advocates for engagement with aesthetic forms—broadly defined as symbols, art, narratives, and performance—as a means of fostering communities committed to practical action in pursuit of justice and the common good.

Teaching Theology in the Time of Ferguson

As a college theology professor, I have the privilege of working with undergraduate students from an array of cultural, political, and religious backgrounds as they encounter Catholic Social Teaching and apply it to the most challenging social issues of our day. In fall 2014, students in my liberation theology class were transfixed by images of racial conflict and protests broadcast daily from Ferguson, Missouri. This tension reached its apex in the Ferguson grand jury's decision not to indict Darren Wilson in connection with the shooting death of Michael Brown. Some students, especially students who had personally experienced racial discrimination, strongly sympathized with Michael Brown. They took to social media with the hashtag #BlackLivesMatter, vociferously declaring their support for the Ferguson protesters. Other students identified with Darren Wilson, especially those preparing for careers in law enforcement. These students had their own hashtag: #BlueLivesMatter, underscoring their support for police officers who stand in harm's way in their duty to serve and protect communities. These hashtags reflect a deep chasm in our responses to the images and stories from Ferguson: some of us saw protests for fundamental human dignity and racial justice; others of us saw riots that endangered police, property, and the rule of law. Our divided classroom community mirrored our polarized society.

These basic differences in perspective could have made for an unproductive semester. Indeed, conversations about race in the context of polarization are always difficult and often frustrating. Yet the students forged a classroom atmosphere of respect, trust, and equality that promoted intellectual discussions about race that were as charitable as they were critical. Thus, the class watched the painful events of that season unfold against the backdrop of our coursework on Catholic social tradition, where we explored the themes of human dignity, preferential option for the poor, social sin, justice, and the common good. These ideas, deeply rooted in Scripture, articulated in Catholic Social Teaching, and elaborated in liberation theology, illustrated a fundamentally human vision of social justice that resonated deeply with the students on either side of the conflict.

This sense of intellectual solidarity empowered the class to confront twenty-first-century manifestations of racism and white supremacy. It even prompted the students to practice dialogue outside of class with an eye toward addressing racial inequality on campus. But this solidarity had limits. Despite the vibrant exchange of ideas, there was still a basic disagreement about what had happened in Ferguson. This disagreement was written into our most formative experiences: whether we were raised to trust or fear law enforcement, whether we were politically liberal or conservative, whether we were theologically traditional or progressive. Students who had been called racial slurs, followed in retail stores, and pulled over by police officers for minor traffic violations did not understand why anyone could side with Darren Wilson. Students preparing to step into the line of fire as law enforcement agents did not understand how anyone could side with Michael Brown. Mirroring US society, the students locked into their own positions. Invariably, our conversations reached a point where they could go no further. This was the point at which our discourse broke down, the impasse at which we no longer "got" our interlocutor's argument.

Aesthetic Solidarity

Intellectual and practical solidarity buckle under the weight of polarization. But in a Catholic Church committed to unity in difference, impasse cannot be the final answer. Solidarity thus requires engagement of human hearts and imaginations toward navigating the challenges of polarization. For this reason, I suggest aesthetic solidarity as a way forward for conversations about racism and racial justice in the Catholic Church.

Theological aesthetics, as defined by theologian Alejandro García-Rivera, concerns "that which moves the human heart."[4] From this perspective, encounters with beauty can shape emotions and imaginations in ways that sustain commitment to common values such as equality, justice, and participation. Aesthetic solidarity thus concerns the formation of community through aesthetic encounter in ways that promote justice. Joining others in acts of aesthetic interpretation can foster solidarity—relationships characterized by mutuality, equality, vulnerability, and participation.[5] This kind of solidarity directs the community formed by beauty toward the pursuit of social justice.

As moral theologian Maureen H. O'Connell explains, aesthetic solidarity forges "imaginative and non-verbal relationality that arises from collective commitments to perceive and cultivate the beauty of persons, communities, and the environment."[6] Engagement with the beautiful—along with the true and the good—promotes the formation of affective bonds, emotions that sustain our commitment to the intellectual and practical tasks of solidarity. Aesthetic solidarity thus adds another dimension to David Hollenbach's conception of intellectual

[4] Alejandro García-Rivera, *The Community of the Beautiful: A Theological Aesthetics* (Collegeville, MN: Liturgical Press, 1999), 9.

[5] See Meghan J. Clark, *The Vision of Catholic Social Thought: The Virtue of Solidarity and the Praxis of Human Rights* (Minneapolis, MN: Fortress, 2014).

[6] Maureen H. O'Connell, *If These Walls Could Talk: Community Muralism and the Beauty of Justice* (Collegeville, MN: Liturgical Press, 2012), 259.

solidarity,[7] in which we strive to know the mind of another, and Lisa Sowle Cahill's emphasis on practical solidarity, where communities unite in action toward the common good.[8]

We should soberly acknowledge that not all communities formed through aesthetic engagement are committed to justice. Indeed, racist movements have often coalesced around aesthetic symbols. Further, aesthetic solidarity is not an antidote to racial polarization in church or society. Racism burrows into personal and social morality in ways that can be difficult to detect and tough to eradicate. Aesthetic solidarity, however, does not aim to "solve" racism. Instead, it strives to inspire further intellectual and practical commitment to the goal of racial justice. Its highest aim is to stir empathy that sustains personal and communal pursuits of social justice. For this reason, aesthetic solidarity is best conceived as a discipline that supports the pursuit of racial justice rather than a solution to racism and white supremacy itself.

The discipline of aesthetic solidarity encourages practices of mindfulness and attention that foster compassion toward others. These practices, bearing affinity with Catholic contemplative traditions, promote attention to human particularity as a means of engaging the other. This particularity is often expressed and encountered through art and beauty: songs, images, performances, poetry, and stories. The discipline of aesthetic solidarity thus calls individuals to expand our perspectives through aesthetic engagement with the other. The decentering practices of mindfulness and attention promote genuine encounter with human difference that can move hearts toward commitment to solidarity and justice.

---

[7] See David Hollenbach, *The Common Good and Christian Ethics* (Cambridge, UK: Cambridge University Press, 2002).

[8] See Lisa Sowle Cahill, *Theological Bioethics: Participation, Justice, and Change*, Moral Traditions (Washington, DC: Georgetown University Press, 2005).

Liturgy and Protest

Catholic liturgy and traditions of social protest illustrate aesthetic solidarity's capacity to cultivate communities committed to justice. The eucharistic liturgy, of course, is the source and summit of the Catholic faith, uniting the Body of Christ across our differences through the encounter with beauty. This liturgy is profoundly aesthetic, engaging every human sense—sight, sound, taste, touch, and smell—in sacramental devotion. Liturgical beauty moves human hearts toward contemplation of the divine mystery, a practice that cultivates mindfulness and attention beyond one's own perspective, broadening human awareness to incorporate God, neighbor, and the whole of creation. The aesthetic encounter of the liturgy thus has the power to unite the believing community in the pursuit of truth and goodness. The encounter with beauty in the Eucharist directs the believer toward commitments to justice and the common good.

The Eucharist, through its communal and aesthetic aspects, protests against dehumanizing practices and systems such as racism and white supremacy. As Copeland explains: "In spatial inclusion, authentic recognition, and humble embrace of different bodies, Eucharistic celebration forms our social imagination, transvalues our values, and transforms the meaning of our human being, of embodying Christ."[9] The aesthetic encounters of the liturgy, then, re-members the Body of Christ that has been dis-membered through abuse and exploitation. The liturgy, then, serves as an act of solidarity with those whose lives are threatened by racist images, ideas, and practices. The Eucharist is the ultimate act of unity with God and with others, calling the church to remember our shared dignity.

Echoing the aesthetic and communal aspects of the eucharistic liturgy, nonviolent social protest offers another crucial

---

[9] M. Shawn Copeland, *Enfleshing Freedom: Body, Race, and Being* (Minneapolis, MN: Fortress 2010), 127.

site for cultivating aesthetic solidarity in our time. Protests for social justice, such as the peaceful ones carried out by community and religious leaders in Ferguson's aftermath, call for practices of mindfulness and attention that draw us toward deeper understanding of a position that may not resonate with our own social sympathies. Witnessing antiracism protests can take one outside of her comfort zone, especially as these protests often employ emphatic, prophetic language and imagery. The goal of these protests, however, is to underscore the unspeakable violence of practices and structures that undermine human dignity. Indeed, the prophetic pursuit of equality, justice, participation, and dignity carries deep meaning in Catholic Social Tradition. Protesters often use music, theater, and poetry to speak out against racial injustice; these signs and symbols call witnesses to attend to the justice claims made by these protests. Protests, like the eucharistic liturgy, thus participate in re-membering the dis-membered Body of Christ. To publically denounce structures that dehumanize racially marginalized people and law enforcement officers alike, the #BlackLivesMatter protesters call on all people of good will to struggle for a more just society in which all humans are treated in accord with their God-given dignity. In this way, both the *act of protesting* and *mindful witness to protest* can be seen as Catholic spiritual disciplines.

Seeing Solidarity

In remembrance of Michael Brown, several students from my liberation theology class organized a "die in" protest, an event during which marchers lie on the ground to symbolize the loss of human life. On a dreary winter day, these students filed silently into a busy dining area where many students and faculty members were eating lunch. Speaking in a loud and clear voice, one of my students called for the crowd's attention. Silence swept across the bustling dining hall. The student proceeded to read statistics about black men killed by police officers before telling the story of Michael Brown's violent death. She described how Brown's lifeless body was left on the pavement on West Florrisant Street in Ferguson for more than four hours. She lamented this as a violation of his human dignity, of the divine gift rooted in the *imago dei* present in him. As she finished her story, she announced that the protestors would lie on the dining hall floor for just over four minutes to represent the hours that Michael Brown's body was left in the street after his death. She invited witnesses to join the protest if they felt so moved. Some students and faculty silently left their lunch trays and joined the protest, gently spreading their bodies across the cool floor tiles.

Some other students from the class were eating lunch in the dining hall during the protest. Two students from class who were preparing for careers in law enforcement sat at a table immediately adjacent to the protest. These students did not join the protest but observed carefully with furrowed brows as their classmates rested lifelessly on the floor. As the minutes ticked away, emotion spread across their faces. At the end of the protest, the protesters silently exited the dining hall and the room filled with noise once again. Yet, these three students sat quietly picking at their meals. I approached the table, asking what they thought of the protest. Their responses:

> "I didn't realize that so many young black men were killed by police officers every year."
> "I didn't realize that Michael Brown was headed to college."
> "Why did his body lay on the ground for so long?"

The protest might not have changed their sympathies, but it did ignite compassion and provoke questions. Their witness to the protest renewed their commitment to the difficult work of addressing racism in the United States. It was a moment of aesthetic solidarity. These students had been transformed from observers into witnesses through aesthetic encounter and practices of mindfulness.

There is no antidote to polarization on issues of race and racism among the church or society today. Yet confronting this problem demands a discipline of aesthetic solidarity that calls forth practices of mindfulness and attention in the context of pluralism. The students in my liberation theology class serve as one model for responding to polarization in the twenty-first-century Catholic Church: openness to beauty and commitment to community can shift the conversation. While what we can learn from aesthetic solidarity in regard to race relations is crucial, the practice can also help to foster empathy and solidarity around other issues driving polarization in both church and public life.

Part 4

Looking to the Future

10

Not Right or Left, Wrong or Right
Millennial Catholics and the Age of Mercy

Elizabeth Tenety

At 2013's World Youth Day in Rio, Pope Francis met the world right where it was.

"What is it that I expect as a consequence of World Youth Day?" Francis said. "I want a mess. We knew that in Rio there would be great disorder, but I want trouble in the dioceses! . . . I want to see the church get closer to the people. I want to get rid of clericalism, the mundane, this closing ourselves off within ourselves, in our parishes, schools, or structures. Because these need to get out!"[1]

For another view into the pope's vision of humanity, take his description of his vision for the church as a "field hospital" in the midst of the world's woundedness. "It is useless to ask a seriously injured person if he has high cholesterol and about the level of his blood sugars! You have to heal his wounds."

Or look at his view of the family. "The perfect family doesn't exist, nor is there a perfect husband or a perfect wife. . . . It's just us sinners."

---

[1] Associated Press, "Pope Urges the Faithful to Make 'A Mess'," *Philly .com*, July 27, 2013, http://articles.philly.com/2013-07-27/news/40817237 _1_pope-francis-catholics-vatican.

In other words, the dynamic leader of the largest religious community on earth sees the church not as a perfect and holy place separate from the world but as an institution at home in the messiness of human life.

And modern human life is as messy as it's ever been.

To examine what this messiness means today, and where the challenges of the twenty-first century will take the church, we can look to the lives of Millennials, that generation born between roughly 1980 and 2000, which is just coming of age in adulthood.

This emerging generation not only has a lot to teach the church but their life experience also begs for a Catholic culture that reaches them with understanding, tenderness, and mercy.

They're skeptical of organized religion. And though Millennials in the United States lean left,[2] particularly on issues of social and economic justice, they overwhelmingly remain "skeptical of the government to do the right thing."[3] With advances in technology moving at a faster pace each year and changes in marriage and childbearing impacting the fundamental structures of their everyday lives, their world is ever evolving. In fact, they expect change.

But rather than being merely a symptom of all that is wrong with the world today, the lives of Millennials are a window into the challenges that the church faces in the twenty-first century—from skepticism of authority to a more open view of the complexities of human sexuality—that Francis himself often seems to be heralding.[4]

[2] *Pew Research Center*, "Q & A: Why Millennials are Less Religious than Older Americans," January 8, 2016, http://www.pewresearch.org /fact-tank/2016/01/08/qa-why-millennials-are-less-religious-than-older -americans/.

[3] Chris Cillizza, "Millennials Don't Trust Anyone. That Is a Big Deal," *Washington Post*, April 30, 2015, https://www.washingtonpost.com/news /the-fix/wp/2015/04/30/millennials-dont-trust-anyone-what-else-is-new/.

[4] Laurie Goodstein, "Pope Francis' Mixed Messages on Sexuality," *New York Times*, July 28, 2015, http://www.nytimes.com/interactive/2015/07/24 /us/29popegaymarriage.html.

And this generation has already faced quite an affront.

Start, for example, with their home lives. Millennials are often critiqued for delaying or devaluing marriage,[5] but for many, that attitude comes from a place of deep pain: older Millennials are children of peak divorce in the late 1970s and early 1980s. While most marriages today are stable, in part because of drastically declining marriage rates among lower income Americans,[6] this generation was born in a world where the central family unit's status was uncertain.

Couple that divorce rate with a defining moment in American public life, and it's easy to see where some of the jadedness comes from: When Millennials were children, they watched the president of the United States be impeached over his definition of sex and whether he had it with a woman who was not his wife. It's one thing to have an awkward coming-of-age conversation with your parents about where babies come from; it's another to be forced to learn about exactly what sex entails by hearing on TV and radio whether or not Bill Clinton *technically* did it with his intern. It was just one more reminder that things are not always what they seem.

Another source of information during the scandal, of course, was just emerging: the Internet. (The scandal grew, in part, because of a new website: The Drudge Report.[7]) Remember, Millennials are the first generation to grow up with this rapidly evolving technology inside their homes—and in many cases knew way more about the workings of the Web than their parents. From dial-up dramas to today's always-on

[5] Tom Keane, "Millennials, Reject Timely Marriage at Your Own Risk," *Boston Globe*, July 27, 2014, https://www.bostonglobe.com/opinion/2014 /07/27/millennials-reject-timely-marriage-your-own-risk/AgCRUNzxN 07BOU4Gn2oISI/story.html.

[6] Claire Cain, "The Divorce Surge Is Over but the Myth Lives On," *New York Times*, December 2, 2014, http://www.nytimes.com/2014/12/02/upshot /the-divorce-surge-is-over-but-the-myth-lives-on.html.

[7] *CNN.com*, January 30, 1998, http://www.cnn.com/ALLPOLITICS /1998/01/30/pandora.web/.

smartphones, this generation developed an understanding that the world, and our connectedness to it, is changing rapidly and often dramatically. Living through this change—where the capabilities of devices used each day improve and evolve with each year—puts a considerable measure of faith in progress and change to make things better. It also casts the recent past in a new "pre-Internet" light. Things that happened not so long ago can still feel dramatically different than today.

Another event divides this generation into two lifetimes: Before 9/11, and after. This was their JFK assassination, their generation's Pearl Harbor. This cast their childhoods against a backdrop of insecurity on the home front and war unfolding abroad.[8] The symbolic attacks in the middle of some of America's largest cities interrupted what was, for many Millennials, one of the first bright days of a brand new school year. On that day, a generation lost its innocence.

Months after 9/11, news of the priest sexual abuse scandal broke out as the Boston Globe capitulated a global wave of allegations and admissions[9] and church reaction and response. If celibacy and the church's teachings on sexuality were viewed as a peculiarity of Catholic life before the scandal, afterward they were often dismissed as dangerous hypocrisy. The impact of the sexual abuse crisis on the mindset of Millennials cannot be understated, and in its wake, many began to believe that the church had no standing to speak to them on issues of sexual ethics. The real and perceived defensiveness of the church in the aftermath further solidified Millennial skepticism.

In the years that followed 9/11, this generation then witnessed the folly of the wars in Iraq and Afghanistan, the miss-

[8] Peter Grier, "How 9/11 Shaped a Generation of Americans," *Christian Science Monitor*, September 9, 2011, http://www.csmonitor.com/USA/Society /2011/0909/How-9-11-has-shaped-a-generation-of-Americans.

[9] Michael Rezendez, "Church Allowed Abuse by Priest for Years," *Boston Globe*, January 6, 2002, https://www.bostonglobe.com/news/special-reports /2002/01/06/church-allowed-abuse-priest-for-years/cSHfGkTIrAT25qKGv BuDNM/story.html.

ing weapons of mass destruction. Their friends and compatriots went off to war—for missions of unclear purpose—and whose impact is still unfolding. (Former British Prime Minister Tony Blair in 2015 admitted that the removal of Saddam Hussein led to the rise of the Islamic State, though he does not regret removing him.) While servicemen and women served heroically, the full impact of their sacrifice remains uncertain. And near the end of the wars, many of the country's celebrated and decorated military leaders fell to scandals of their own making.

Millennials have also grown up in an era of mass shootings—from Columbine to Virginia Tech, to Newtown—that make many of them feel insecure even in spaces that should be safe. As a country, there are predictable "national conversations" and feelings of outrage and hopelessness each time but no sense that anything will ever really change. Americans feel unsafe even in the most innocent of places.[10]

And over the last ten years, we've watched the last throes of the culture wars in the battle over gay rights and same-sex marriage. Today, 73 percent of Millennials support same-sex marriage, according to a 2015 study by the Pew Research Center.[11] This generation that grew up in a world where "gay" was flung around as an insult now sees gay rights as an issue they overwhelmingly accept. The church's official teaching on marriage is not as bothersome for many Millennials as is its lobbying to keep gay couples from obtaining full legal rights. And today they watch as the church's top leaders tear one another apart over how to mete out mercy to gay people and their families.

[10] Alice Bidwell, "Fighting, Guns Down, but More Students Feel Unsafe at School," *U.S. News and World Report*, June 16, 2014, http://www.usnews.com/news/blogs/data-mine/2014/06/16/fighting-guns-down-at-schools-but-more-students-feel-unsafe.

[11] *Pew Research Center*, "Support for Same-Sex Marriage at Record High, but Key Segments Remain Opposed," June 8, 2015, http://www.people-press.org/2015/06/08/support-for-same-sex-marriage-at-record-high-but-key-segments-remain-opposed/.

This is the culture that has shaped the Millennial generation. These are the wounds and the experiences they bare.
We often hear in religious circles that the beliefs and values
of Millennials represent a move away from the traditional
Christianity. Yet, when I hear people criticizing powerful institutions for their hypocrisy, rejecting rigidity, asking "Who
am I judge?"—we don't just hear the mantra of Millennials. I
believe we hear the words of Jesus.

This is why Pope Francis has been so wildly well-received
by Millennial Catholics. This supremely quotable pope; this
pope who criticizes the clergy, who isn't afraid to dine with
sinners—or wash their feet. This pope who isn't afraid to make
a mess, to pick at orthodoxies around topics like Communion
for the divorced or to find new ways to meet people amid the
imperfections of real life. The pope who wants to lead with
mercy rather than judgment. That's what Catholic Millennials
love. That's what all Millennials need.

This pope reminds people of Christ. He reminds Millennials
of what they love about Christianity—or at least, the Christian
story. It's a story of hope amid brokenness. Of choosing to heal
the sick on the Sabbath day. Of rejecting the "way it's supposed
to be done" for the way it needs to be now.

The church can move forward when it learns from the life
experience of Millennials instead of blaming them for not living
up to some pristine ideal. They inherited a broken world, and
they've learned to deal with complexities with compassion.
For this generation, nonjudgmental solidarity is a way of life.

Pope Francis has shown a path—not the only path—but
an important one, for the church to take. A church that is in
love with mercy and grace isn't busy worrying about who is
in, or who is out, or whom they should judge. They just love
one another. They just exemplify the way.

11

Polarization and Abortion
Living Out Our Pro-Life Beliefs

Erin Stoyell-Mulholland

The issue of increased polarization within the Catholic Church in the United States cannot be adequately addressed without discussing abortion. This contentious topic is often associated with strong feelings, heated rhetoric, and extremist positions. Many Catholics choose not to engage in any discussions surrounding abortion, avoiding the debate by saying: "I don't have a strong opinion," or "I wouldn't do that, but I can't tell others how to live." In this chapter, I reflect on how the issue of abortion has contributed to the polarization that the church experiences today and how Millennials respond to this polarization. I offer my own personal experience within this polarized climate, and how I, and other pro-life leaders, took steps to further the pro-life cause by reducing the way the pro-life movement contributes to polarization. I conclude by offering practical suggestions on how we, the church, can decrease the polarizing effects of the abortion debate and foster the development of a culture of life. In this reflection, I write through the lens of my own experience and with the recognition that everyone has their own experiences.

One of the most important lessons learned through the Notre Dame conference from which this volume comes is the necessity of having difficult conversations such as those concerning abortion. In order to seek truth in love, we must be willing to dialogue with those we disagree with, regardless of how difficult or painful that conversation might be. Pope Benedict XVI writes, "In Christ, charity in truth becomes the Face of his Person, a vocation for us to love our brothers and sisters in the truth of his plan."[1] By seeking the truth *in love*, we are imitating Christ and fulfilling our true vocation. This is important when discussing all aspects of church teaching but can become particularly poignant when addressing tough issues such as abortion.

More importantly, we cannot ignore the reality of lived experiences. Abortion has been legal in the United States for over forty years. Abortion is not a theoretical issue or an issue that only some people deal with. Abortion is a very personal issue that has touched each and every person in this nation, whether they recognize it or not. Each individual's understanding of abortion is influenced by their experiences surrounding abortion, even if they do not recognize how abortion has impacted their life.

Before we begin this important conversation on how the Catholic Church can and should live out its pro-life values through opposition to abortion, it's important to acknowledge these experiences. Many men and women in this country are suffering from the tragedy of abortion. In a meta-analysis of studies done on abortion and mental health, the results found that women who had abortions were 81 percent more likely to have mental health problems.[2] Many of these men and women affected by abortion sit in the pews with us on Sunday. This is

---

[1] Benedict XVI, Encyclical Letter *Caritas in Veritate*, June 29, 2009, http://w2.vatican.va/content/benedict-xvi/en/encyclicals/documents/hf_ben-xvi_enc_20090629_caritas-in-veritate.html.

[2] Priscilla K. Coleman, "Abortion and Mental Health: A Quantitative Synthesis and Analysis of Research Published, 1995–2009," *British Journal of Psychiatry* 199, no. 3 (August 2011).

a fact we must be cognizant of as we continue this conversation and have these conversations with others. We must always look to understand a person's story. A person's story will tell you much more than his ideology ever could. The following story illustrates the polarization that can occur when having these important conversations about abortion.

For years, Notre Dame's Right to Life club erected a Cemetery of the Innocents on campus during Respect Life Week. This display consisted of hundreds of white crosses scattered across South Quad, with signs indicating that these crosses represented all the lives that had been lost to abortion. This display caused quite a controversy on campus, even being vandalized one year. The contentious response and vandalization of the crosses only served to solidify Right to Life's leaders thinking that the display was necessary. So, every year, the display went up. By the time I arrived on campus as a freshman, however, I believed that the cemetery was no longer accomplishing its purpose. As a member of Right to Life, I understood the reasoning of the cemetery. I saw that it was meant to honor and memorialize all the lives lost to abortion. Most students on campus, however, did not see it that way. Instead, most students saw it as a judgment or condemnation of those women who chose to have abortions. Even some pro-life students felt that the way the pro-life message was being communicated through the crosses was not helpful to the pro-life cause.

When I became president of Notre Dame Right to Life in my junior year, my team and I started to brainstorm ways to portray the same pro-life message but in a different way. This was not met without protest. A friend told me that he could no longer respect me as a leader if I got rid of the cemetery. Others grumbled about me "softening" the message, both publicly and privately. I even had one club member tell me that I was "removing the last beacon of hope" at Notre Dame. Still, I firmly believed that we could find a better way to portray the pro-life message, and we found a way to do so. In place of the cemetery, we choose to display a garden of white and red intertwined roses. Each white rose represented a life lost due to abortion. The red roses represented those who have suffered emotionally, spiritually, and physically because of abortion, including mothers, fathers, families, and friends. The garden was centered around a cross, the source of hope and healing for all.

With these roses, we sought to raise the same awareness of the effects of abortion and commemorate the lives lost while simultaneously extending a deeper invitation to love. The flowers demonstrated the fragility, beauty, and value of every human life. We acknowledged there are many students on college campuses who have been affected by abortion, both directly and indirectly. The display was a loving way of reaching out to acknowledge those wounds and offer hope for healing. It was an invitation to the entire community to join together in promoting a greater respect for the dignity of all life.

I believe the unique difference in this display is that it both acknowledges and offers hope and healing to all those who have been affected by abortion. The day the garden went up, I got an e-mail from a senior student on campus. She wrote to me saying as she biked past the signs she read, *"For all those affected by abortion.* I was now a part of this memorial; my affair had been commemorated. The pain flooded back, along with a peculiar anger."* This woman had not had an abortion, but she had been personally affected by it, just as we all have been affected by abortion, whether we know it or not. When she saw the garden, she recognized this. Although initially her reaction was one of anger and grief, through reaching out via e-mail, she was able to engage in further conversation which allowed her to more fully confront what had happened. This is what we sought to do with this garden. Although the wide-reaching impact of abortion is not a comfortable fact, it is a reality. It is only through confronting this uncomfortable reality that we are able to take steps forward.

On college campuses especially, it is important to remember that many women and men are suffering from the wounds of abortion. Although we do not want to keep silent on this issue, it is important to keep these people in mind when doing pro-life activism. Truth needs to be spread with love, not merely facts or statistics. The roses commemorate the pain of these individuals while providing an opportunity for the rest of campus to engage in discussion.

This story not only exemplifies the importance of the manner in which the pro-life message is presented but also offers a way forward for the Catholic Church on one most polarizing issues of our time. According to Guttmacher, 28 percent of women receiving abortions identify as Catholic—and given the meta-analysis cited earlier, we can be confident that many millions of Catholics are suffering from the effects of abortion. Millennials don't want to see judgment and condemnation. Many think that the church has not done a good enough job defending and celebrating each and every life. Millennials embrace the pro-life movement when they believe it is about defending and celebrating all human life. Here, we find a beautiful opportunity for the church to be a leader in this vision of what it means to be pro-life: supporting women *and* children. Young people are sick of "battle imagery" when it comes to the pro-life movement. This is one of the reasons that I think the cemetery lost its impact. The white crosses were reminiscent of a war memorial—an image that is not compelling to young people. Christian Smith noted earlier in this volume that Millennials are sick of culture wars and the polarization that comes with them.[3] A study on Millennials' values found that a majority of Millennials see Christianity as being too judgmental. This same study found that a slim majority of Millennials believe abortion to be morally wrong.[4] It is not the message that Millennials disagree with, it's the way that this message

[3] See Christian Smith's reflection in this volume, p. 16.

[4] Public Religion Research Institute and Georgetown University's Berkley Center for Religion, Peace, and World Affairs, "Survey | A Generation in Transition: Religion, Values, and Politics among College-Age Millennials,"

is being portrayed. When speaking out against abortion turns into an "us versus them" mentality, you lose the interest of young people. Young people do not want to destroy a culture of death. That is not a compelling mission. But when we talk about supporting and loving a pregnant woman and her child, young people want to get involved. When the message is a message of love, not a message of judgment, people are drawn to the pro-life movement. When we call others to think outside of themselves, to join us in building up a culture of life, then we have the attention of young people.

Millennials also do not want to be told what not to do, particularly when it comes to personal issues. "Don't have sex outside marriage." "Don't support the legalization of gay marriage." "Don't have an abortion." When Millennials see the church's teachings as a list of "do nots," this does not lead them to want to embrace the church and her teachings. The pro-life message must be seen and portrayed as a beautiful vision for the future, not something else they are told not to do. When young people are invited into building a future, building up a culture of life, this is when they become excited and animated. Elizabeth Tenety points out that Millennials grew up in a great time of distrust that has led us to become skeptical of authority. She noted that we are drawn to Pope Francis because he reminds us of Christ, that he reminds us of love.[5] This love that Pope Francis models for us can be seen in efforts to build up a culture of life.

This message of love is not only a philosophy but, at its core, is also a way of life. There are a number of concrete actions that can be taken to spread this message of love: Through expanding pregnancy resources on college campuses so that no student has to choose between her child and her education. Through supporting maternity and paternity leave in the

Public Religion Research Institute, December 31, 2015, http://publicreligion .org/site/wp-content/uploads/2012/04/Millennials-Survey-Report.pdf.

[5] See Elizabeth Tenety's remarks in this book, p. 113.

workplace so that families can have a proper work-life balance. By hosting diaper-drives at our local parishes to provide diapers for those who would not otherwise be able to afford them. These are concrete actions that we as a church can take to affirm life. By showing that the church is truly pro-life and not just pro-birth, we both affirm the beauty of the church's teachings and deliver their message through love. Pope St. John Paul II writes:

> Every Christian community, with a renewed sense of responsibility, must continue to write this history through various kinds of pastoral and social activity. To this end, appropriate and effective programmes of support for new life must be implemented, with special closeness to mothers who, even without the help of the father, are not afraid to bring their child into the world and to raise it.[6]

The church recognizes that a culture of life must be supported by a culture of care for neighbor at every stage of life. This is not merely a suggestion, but our responsibility as Christians.

This also means recognizing that abortion is not and must not be a partisan issue. Being pro-life does not mean aligning with a particular political party. As pro-life Catholics, we should be encouraging our politicians and lawmakers in both political parties to support bills and policies that build up a culture of life. By aligning ourselves solely with one party or another because of its position on abortion, we are not truly embracing what it means to be pro-life in its entirety. Currently, people tend to associate the Republican Party with the pro-life effort. But when citizens who prioritize pro-life legislation associate that legislation with one political party, widespread and substantial progress cannot occur. We need to advocate for all our politicians to take a stand and defend life in all its stages.

---

[6] John Paul II, Encyclical Letter, *Evangelium Vitae*, December 2, 2015, http://w2.vatican.va/content/john-paul-ii/en/encyclicals/documents/hf _jp-ii_enc_25031995_evangelium-vitae.html.

This does not stop at simply advocating for restrictions on abortion. As Catholics, we should be encouraging our politicians to create an environment in which abortion is not just illegal, but unthinkable. We need to create safety nets for women in crisis pregnancies so that a pregnancy does not seem like an end to her future and to her dreams. The politicians that we advocate for should be supporting measures like mandatory paid maternity leave. Pro-life politicians should be advocating for an end to pregnancy discrimination in the workplace. They should advocate for better access to prenatal care and more affordable childcare. These are all measures that would help to build up a culture where abortion does not seem like the only option for many women. As Catholics, we should be encouraging this holistic view of being pro-life. We should not settle for candidates who say that they are pro-life and do nothing about it.

The separation of life issues from social justice issues is a serious cause of polarization in the Catholic Church. I think as the church we very frequently see these issues as two distinct and separate things. People seem to believe that they can either fight to eradicate poverty, or they can fight for the rights of the unborn. Not only can they been seen as two completely separate issues but also, oftentimes, they can be pitted against one another.

- "Well, if you truly want to eliminate abortion, you should be working on reducing poverty, because reducing poverty reduces abortions."
- "Well, if you really respect the dignity of every individual, you will recognize that the mass killing of over a million children a year is more important."
- "Don't the children who are already born deserve more of our time and resources? Most women who choose abortion already have kids. They won't bring more kids into this world if their other children are impoverished."
- "So letting women kill their own children is preferable to children being in poverty?"

Arguments like this are common among Catholics. Instead of finding common ground, people will argue about what is more important and how to go about seeking the common good.

Demonizing other people's passions simply has to stop. One of the beautiful things about the Catholic Church is the depth and breadth of our Catholic Social Teaching. Fighting poverty and fighting abortion are not issues that should be either/ or but issues that go hand in hand. The United States Conference of Catholic Bishops wrote a document laying out the seven key principles of Catholic Social Teaching. Each of these "principles build on the foundation of Catholic social teaching: the dignity of human life. This central Catholic principle requires that we measure every policy, every institution, and every action by whether it protects human life and enhances human dignity, especially for the poor and vulnerable."[7] We need organizations that are focused on feeding the homeless. We need organizations that advocate for immigration reform. And we need organizations that are committed to fighting the tragedy of abortion.

One way this separation between social justice issues and pro-life issues can be clearly seen is at both a diocesan and parish level. If you look at the organization of diocesan offices, oftentimes there is a pro-life office and a separate social justice office. These are seen and viewed as two very different and distinct offices. They may fight for resources and funding. One office may feel much more appreciated than the other, and too often these diocesan offices are pitted against one another. I believe this is a major roadblock to accomplishing the goals of both offices. Similarly, in parishes, there are often "Respect Life" groups and "Social Concerns" groups, which have very little interaction with each other.

---

[7] United States Catholic Bishops, *Sharing Catholic Social Teaching: Challenges and Directions*, http://www.usccb.org/beliefs-and-teachings /what-we-believe/catholic-social-teaching/sharing-catholic-social-teaching -challenges-and-directions.cfm.

The diocese of Camden takes a different approach. This is how they describe their office:

> Here in the Diocese of Camden, there is no Respect Life Office. There is no Justice and Peace Office. Instead, we have what we're calling "Life & Justice Ministries." The ampersand—&—in the title is the most important part: it unites our efforts on behalf of human life and social justice. They are impossible to separate. We are called to protecting human life and dignity from the moment of conception onward, all the way to natural death, including *every moment in between*. As Cardinal Timothy Dolan of New York said, "The Ampersand means we are called to care for the 'uns': the *un*-employed; the *un*-insured; the *un*-wanted; the *un*-wed mother, and her innocent, fragile *un*-born baby in her womb; the *un*-documented; the *un*-housed; the *un*-healthy; the *un*-fed; the *under*-educated."[8]

This is how the diocese of Camden sees the pro-life message as being consistent with social justice issues. In fact, not only consistent but also necessary for them to go hand in hand. This could be a model for the church. By not only saying that all life issues are connected but also showing this through our actions and the way in which we organize our dioceses, we would be sending a very powerful message. I believe that through these efforts, we will see a lessening of the polarization surrounding the pro-life message.

The name of this compilation is "Polarization in the US Catholic Church: Naming the Wounds, Beginning to Heal." Naming the wounds is a good place to start. But simply identifying the places that we, as a church, are hurting is not enough. In order to truly begin to heal, we must first acknowledge these wounds but then seek to take concrete actions to restore trust in our community. Throughout this book, we have discussed

---

[8] "Why 'The Ampersand'?," The Ampersand: Diocese of Camden Life & Justice Ministries, December 5, 2012, https://camdenlifejustice.wordpress.com/why-the-ampersand/.

the importance of parish life in this healing process. I believe that understanding the important role that parishes can take in decreasing polarization in the church is an important first step. Systematic change rarely comes from a top-down approach. It is through building communities and cultures that encourage respectful dialogue with whom we disagree that we can begin to see other people's opinions and experiences. One of the conference participants remarked that we should want to go to Mass alongside those who make our blood boil. I agree.

The debate on abortion—and the polarization it has caused—has now entered its fifth decade. Sometimes, it might seem easier to just give up or to avoid these tough conversations. But our faith calls us to something more. The church calls us to witness to the truth as Christ did—through love. It is because we love our neighbor that we must engage in these tough conversations and create an environment where all life is welcomed with love. It is because we love our fellow parishioner sitting in the pew next to us that we not only speak with love but also listen with love.

Being pro-life and standing against the tragedy of abortion should not be a polarizing force in the Catholic Church. But because we have done such a poor job of listening for the past forty years—particularly to those with different points of view—it has become one of the most polarizing issues in the church. This can be remedied. People of opposing viewpoints need to be willing to truly listen to each other. We can truly model Christ and pursue the truth in love. This is what Christ calls us to do, and this is what the church has been calling us to do. We need to respond accordingly.

12

The Unheeded Middle

Catholic Conservative-Liberal Polarities in an Increasingly Hispanic Church

Hosffman Ospino

"What is your position?" asked the professor in a gradu-ate seminar in theology I was enrolled in nearly two decades ago, discussing what I soon learned was a polarizing issue for many Catholics in the United States: immigration reform. "Liberal, or conservative?" the professor continued. The either/or question caught me off guard. I was in my early twenties, having recently migrated from Latin America, and was barely starting to figure out my place in US society and the world of American Catholicism. What exactly he meant by "liberal" or "conservative" was somewhat beyond my grasp at the time. Based on the conversation, it was evident that my classmates, all US-born, non-Hispanic, comfortably argued from one side or the other of this conversation, strangely reducing it to a zero sum equation. They had grown up with this language. Much of this was quite new for me. Maybe I was too young. Being Hispanic and Catholic, however—and an immigrant—made the question personal.

Though I could not spend much time developing a sophis-ticated response to the question, there were some principles rooted in my faith that informed my thought about this reality: all human beings, regardless of their migratory status, possess an inalienable dignity; Catholic immigrants are an integral presence in the life of the church in the United States; the presence of immigrants is a unique opportunity for the church in this country to advance its evangelizing mission in creative ways and, in turn, be evangelized. These are deeply ecclesiological principles. Was such line of thought "liberal" or "conservative"? I could not tell. But instinctively resisting to reduce reality to simplistic categories, I answered: "I stand with the Christian tradition." Yes, the unfolding Christian tradition discerned through our shared historical continuum *in the Church* and *with the Church* as the People of God.[1] Today, I am much more aware of the context, meaning, and debates associated with "liberal" and "conservative" categories. They permeate almost every single conversation in our faith communities, from how to celebrate the liturgy and read the Scriptures to how to raise children or live one's sexuality.

Boundaries and Casualties of Polarization

Christianity is no stranger to polarization. Throughout the centuries, Christian communities have engaged in various readings of the shared elements of the faith tradition with particular nuances. Early in the history of the Christian communities, for instance, the famous schools of thought in Antioch and Alexandria embodied different approaches to much of Christian life. This was evident when reading the Scriptures and interpreting the mystery of Jesus Christ. Scholars associated with the school of Antioch tended to favor a more literal reading of the Scriptures and strongly emphasized the Logos-human dimension of Jesus Christ (Jesus as a human person). Those associated with the school of Alexandria promoted

---

[1] Every conversation about polarization in the Church in our day should start with a prayerful reading of Vatican II's constitutions, starting with *Lumen Gentium*, the Dogmatic Constitution on the Church.

the use of allegory to read the Bible (i.e., establishing creative spiritual and theological connections among images from the Old Testament and the New Testament) and emphasized the mystery of the Logos who becomes flesh.[2] One perspective did not necessarily exclude the other. At points, the perspectives embodied by these schools were taken to extremes, leading to some confusion and divisions, which called for correction. A variety of councils, along with the work of pastors and theologians, building on the energy of the debates and, guided by a profound ecclesial, spiritual, and pastoral mind, provided pathways to move forward.

There are many other examples of polarization in the history of Christian communities as these communities set out to interpret the experience of Jesus Christ and his paschal mystery. Christianity in the East, with its rich variety of rites, would take a slightly different path compared to Christianity in the West. The rich spiritual tradition of the Desert Fathers, who chose a life of radical prayer and isolation, was soon counterbalanced by the rise of monastic life that favored life in community. Monastic life, in turn, would be reformed several times to adjust to the needs of the time or to return to an original vision. The rise of religious orders would introduce ways of living the Gospel in community while embracing a particular charism, usually outside of the community. These orders would evolve over time through reforms and adaptations. The art of theological reflection would transition from almost an exclusive focus on biblical commentary to the use of philosophy— and later, other fields of knowledge. Since the early 1500s, expressions of Catholic Christianity shaped prior to the Council of Trent would take root and thrive in Latin America for several centuries, while another set of expressions developed after Trent would characterize Catholicism in Europe and North

[2] See Justo L. González, *A History of Christian Thought: From the Beginnings to the Council of Chalcedon* (Nashville, TN: Abingdon Press, 1987), 186–226, 335–52.

America.[3] The Christian Catholic experience is richer, stronger, and more dynamic because of these emphases and approaches to living out the Christian message. Even when excesses have come close to introducing division, a profound ecclesial, spiritual, and pastoral spirit seems to have prevailed.

Many of our conversations in the church today echo those of earlier Christians. The tensions are similar, as are the values at stake. The difference is that we have these conversations in the particularity of our own sociohistorical location. The acknowledgment of this reality should bring peace to our minds, reminding us that this is part of what it means to be human and Christian. We discuss and debate our faith because we care about it. And just as those Catholic sisters and brothers before us chose to work toward forms of communion rooted in the truth and the best of the Gospel, we have a responsibility to do likewise. Among the most painful moments in the history of Christianity have been those that led to the brokenness of ecclesial communion, leaving the entire body of believers longing for healing and peace among sisters and brothers.[4]

American Catholics, regardless of our race and social location, live, practice, and debate our faith in the particular context of the United States sociocultural matrix. We are both American and Catholic. We must be constantly attentive to how much influence this context has on our own perceptions and how it shapes our language and interactions. Most importantly, we must beware of embracing forms of ideological

[3] See Orlando O. Espín, *The Faith of the People: Theological Reflections on Popular Catholicism* (Maryknoll, NY: Orbis Books, 1997), 177.

[4] See John Paul II, Encyclical Letter *Ut Unum Sint* (On Commitment to Ecumenism), May 25, 1995, http://w2.vatican.va/content/john-paul-ii/en /encyclicals/documents/hf_jp-ii_enc_25051995_ut-unum-sint.html, 2, 6, 22; Francis, Apostolic Exhortation *Evangelii Gaudium* (On the Proclamation of the Gospel in Today's World), November 24, 2013, https://w2.vatican.va /content/francesco/en/apost_exhortations/documents/papa-francesco _esortazione-ap_20131124_evangelii-gaudium.html, 244–46.

polarization that are devoid of Christian charity and a deep sense of ecclesial communion.

Our society as a whole seems to be engulfed in polarizing battles that continue to fuel the so-called culture wars.[5] On the surface, these battles ride on the two-party scheme that dominates our political system, leaving little room for political alternatives that are viable and credible. Such a scheme forces US citizens to approach politics from an either/or perspective (liberal versus conservative, in this case) and to side, consciously or unconsciously, with particular interests that each side proposes—even when the ideological platforms and commitments that supposedly identify each side are constantly shifting.[6] On a deeper level, polarization in US society appears to be the expression of a radical (postmodern?) individualism that privileges a culture of unrestricted choice and self-interest, usually at the expense of the community in any of its expressions (e.g., family, neighborhood, church), the common good, and love for one another.[7] As indicated above, we are children of our society.

Radical forms of polarization can be destructive, especially those that close their doors to dialogue and ignore the possibility of an ultimate end. In the context of the church, the most

[5] For a sociological analysis on the culture wars and the origins of this category, see the still-relevant work of James Davison Hunter, *Culture Wars: The Struggle to Define America* (New York: Basic Books, 1991). For a more recent analysis of the phenomenon in the context of American Catholicism, see Mary Ellen Konieczny, *The Spirit's Tether: Family, Work, and Religion among American Catholics* (New York: Oxford University Press, 2013).

[6] A great analysis of shifting allegiances among the two main political parties and the religious undertone associated of those shifts is insightfully presented in sociologist William V. D'Antonio's work *Religion, Politics, and Polarization: How Religiopolitical Conflict Is Changing Congress and American Democracy* (Lanham, MD: Rowman & Littlefield), 2013.

[7] See Roberto S. Goizueta, "Rationality or Irrationality: Modernity, Postmodernity, and the U.S. Hispanic Theologian," chap. 6 in *Caminemos con Jesús: Toward a Hispanic/Latino Theology of Accompaniment* (Maryknoll, NY: Orbis Books, 1995).

immediate casualty of such forms of polarization is ecclesial communion with one another. Radical forms of polarization are also inherently and dangerously exclusionary. One may get the impression that people in our society—and in our church—are equally divided among those on side A and side B of any issue, "liberals" and "conservatives" if we want to use this language, thus getting the impression that most tensions lead to a zero-sum conclusion or a stalemate. But this is a naive impression. Though it is almost inescapable that we live amid some form of tension, since most things are rarely black or white, the polarized extremes, regardless of their side, are a rather small cross section of the whole—about 20 percent or so![8]

There is a large middle; the unheeded middle. Many in it resist discerning reality exclusively as either/or, preferring instead a both/and outlook that freely incorporates variations of the sides of polarization. Their lives are defined not by the outcomes of the culture wars but by responding to the immediate demands that shape everyday existence. Millions of them in the United States are silent immigrants or children of immigrants negotiating identities every second of their lives in order to survive, yet are ignored by loud, dominant voices that often presuppose biased forms of assimilation and remain apathetic as their sisters and brothers vanish in a sea of anonymity. In the unheeded middle, we encounter countless young people who do care about their spiritual journeys and see life with renewed hope but don't want to fight the polarizing battles of their elders and the most outspoken voices in a divided society/church. Those in this middle find the polarization of the extremes toxic and disheartening, unworthy of committing their time and energy. Though not ideal, indifference and lack of involvement emerge as serious alternatives for them. The middle drifts away. They are the largest casualty of radical polarization.

[8] See the interesting work and compelling analysis of Jonathan Haidt, *The Righteous Mind: Why Good People Are Divided by Politics and Religion* (New York: Pantheon Books), 2012.

As we can see, polarization is not only about the tension between "left" and "right" but also between center and margins. In this case, the center does not seem to be one of power but the large and unheeded middle. The margins are the polarized extremes that permanently push boundaries outward, as if they had outgrown a middle that they don't seem to need anymore.

Drifting Away

US Catholicism began the twenty-first century amid a series of major transformations that are redefining its identity, priorities, and commitments. One phenomenon that raises much concern among pastoral leaders in our day is the long and sustained process of defection from Catholic ranks during the last few decades. All in all, 32 million Catholics have stopped self-identifying as such in the United States.[9] The sociocultural milieu that allowed Catholic communities to thrive during the nineteenth and early twentieth centuries has dramatically changed. The widespread influence of forces such as globalization, relativism, and secularism, among others, poses major challenges to core assumptions and practices that identify Catholicism. It is as if US Catholics have been suddenly rendered unable to communicate and connect with one another, especially with our young and the new immigrants. Thousands of our parishes and schools are closing; thriving programs and organizations are coming to the end of their life cycle.

Polarized extremes quickly emerge to explain what is happening. "Liberal" voices blame conservative ones for not adjusting quickly to the demands of a fast-changing society, for holding back, for suppressing creativity. In fact, many of those who have left the church see themselves holding more liberal views. "Conservative" voices blame liberal ones for diluting

---

[9] See Mark Gray, "Lapsed Catholics Weigh In on Why They Left Church," *Our Sunday Visitor*, October 22, 2014, https://www.osv.com/OSVNews weekly/Story/TabId/2672/ArtMID/13567/ArticleID/16269/Lapsed-Catholics -weigh-in-on-why-they-left-Church.aspx.

what is perceived to be a given identity, for introducing change where change should not happen, for not being resolutely countercultural. And so the blame game goes. Each side draws clear lines. Some look at the past with the hope for certain restoration. Others anticipate the future for glimpses of what they don't yet see. The battlegrounds vary: the liturgy, questions about life, family, sexuality, poverty, theological reflection, etc. An either/or approach to discuss those complex realities is taken for granted. Pundits, experts, and authorities on both sides write, blog, and teach. In the meantime, 32 million Catholics have exited the door.

But perhaps the most influential and permanent factor redefining the entire American Catholic experience is the demographic transition taking place at the grassroots levels in our faith communities. Only half a century ago, about 90 percent of all US Catholics were Euro-American, white. The presence of Asian, black, Hispanic, and Native American Catholics was quite small. Today, the face of the church in the United States looks significantly different. Asians constitute 5 percent of the US Catholic population and are the fastest growing group in our church. Large numbers of Black Catholic immigrants have made the United States their home in recent decades, expanding and enriching the American black Catholic experience. The Native American Catholic presence remains small (about 1 percent), yet steady. The bulk of the demographic transformation, however, comes from the Hispanic sector of the church. About 43 percent of Catholics in the country are Hispanic. More interestingly, about 60 percent of US Catholics under eighteen share a Hispanic background. In large regions of the country, particularly the Southwest and major urban areas, Hispanics are the majority of the US Catholic population. Hispanics account for 71 percent of the growth of the Catholic population in the United States since 1960.[10]

---

[10] See Hosffman Ospino, *Hispanic Ministry in Catholic Parishes: A Summary Report of Findings from the National Study of Catholic Parishes with Hispanic Ministry*, Bilingual ed., English and Spanish (Huntington, IN: Our Sunday Visitor), 2015. Also available online at www.bc.edu/stmhispanicparishstudy. For a detailed

These demographic changes are real. They bring fresh cultural, linguistic, and even spiritual perspectives. They also bring new challenges that call for a reorganization of priorities and commitments in our local communities and the work of our dioceses and organizations.

Hispanic Catholics are present in every diocese of the United States, even in those where no formal Hispanic ministry has been established at the parochial or diocesan levels. Though the number of Hispanics who self-identify as Catholics has decreased in the last couple of decades, a strong 58 percent of the nearly 60 million US Hispanics do so. Because most practicing Catholics are affiliated with a parish community, parishes serve as a good indicator to measure the vitality and direction of Catholic life in a particular society. About 26 percent of all parishes in the United States (about 17,337 in 2015) have developed some form of Hispanic ministry, generally defined as ministry to the Spanish-speaking and their families. But this general definition of Hispanic ministry paints a limited picture. Most Hispanic Catholics are also English-speaking and about two-thirds are US born. Thus, parishes are quickly adjusting to serving a Catholic population that is strongly bilingual, with a large immigrant portion (about 20 million Hispanics are immigrants) raising and passing on the faith—and their culture—to the largest segment of the next generation of US Catholics. Looking closely at the life of parishes with Hispanic ministry provides us with a picture of what is affecting the ecclesial lives of about half of US Catholics.[11] Here are a few

---

analysis of the contemporary Hispanic Catholic experience, see Timothy M. Matovina, *Latino Catholicism: Transformation in America's Largest Church* (Princeton, NJ: Princeton University Press, 2012). From the perspective of Hispanic ministry see Hosffman Ospino, ed., *Hispanic Ministry in the 21st Century: Present and Future* (Miami, FL: Convivium Press, 2010), and Hosffman Ospino, Elsie Miranda, and Brett Hoover, eds., *Hispanic Ministry in the 21st Century: Urgent Matters* (Miami, FL: Convivium Press, 2016).

[11] See Hosffman Ospino, *Hispanic Ministry in Catholic Parishes*, 42–44.

overarching dynamics impacting US Hispanic Catholic life in parishes learned through a recent research project I had the privilege to conduct as its principal investigator, namely, the *National Study of Catholic Parishes with Hispanic Ministry.*

1. Socio-Ecclesial Location

Most parishes with Hispanic ministry are located in urban settings and serve large populations of Hispanics who constantly struggle with poverty, lack access to basic social benefits (e.g., healthcare, quality education, decent housing, good paying jobs), and are often subjected to biases such as racism and classism. Hundreds of parishes with Hispanic ministry are located in neighborhoods where violence and at risk conditions are widespread. Although not all Hispanics are poor or undocumented, many are: about a quarter of Hispanics live in poverty and another quarter very near the poverty level. Close to 10 million Hispanics are undocumented. Parishes are, for many of these Catholics, oases for hope and opportunity.

2. Pastoral Agency

The number of Hispanic pastoral leaders in decision-making positions in the church in the United States is very small compared to the size of the population. Barely 10 percent of bishops, 6 percent of Catholic school teachers and administrators, 6 percent of priests, 6 percent of sisters, and 6 percent of Catholic theologians are Hispanic. The vast majority of Hispanic priests (8 of 10) and sisters (9.5 of 10) are foreign born. Though half of all Catholics enrolled in lay ecclesial ministry programs are estimated to be Hispanic, only 17 percent are in programs leading toward a degree.[12] The levels of underrepresentation in Catholic parishes, dioceses, institutions, and organizations

---

[12] See Center for Applied Research in the Apostolate (CARA), *Research Review: Lay Ecclesial Ministers in the United States* (Washington, DC: CARA, 2015), 9–10, http://cara.georgetown.edu/lemsummit.pdf.

place Hispanics in positions of disadvantage to advocate for specific evangelization resources and services needed in their communities. Their voices do not have enough platforms to share the rich spiritual, theological, and pastoral contributions to the life of the church that they bring.

3. Hispanic Youth

Three in five US Catholics under the age of eighteen are Hispanic. That is about 8 million young Catholics. About 93 percent of them are US born. One would imagine that dioceses, parishes, schools, and other institutions at the service of the church's evangelizing mission in this country would have already shifted large amounts of resources to invest in the next generation of American Catholics. Yet we are far from that ideal. Only 40 percent of parishes with Hispanic ministry have programs directly serving Hispanic youth. These are the communities that would be most likely to have such programs, since the other two-thirds of parishes are not known for directly serving this population. Merely 3 percent of school-age Hispanic children—only 300,000—are enrolled in Catholic schools. Enrollment of Hispanic students continues to move at a very slow pace. Yet, the closing of Catholic schools sadly happens much faster than anyone desires. Between the year 2000 and 2015, 26 percent of existing Catholic schools closed. More than 7,000 Catholic schools have closed during the last half-century. Only 10 percent of Hispanic Catholic children are enrolled in programs of religious education in parishes with Hispanic ministry.[13]

What does all this have to do with polarization in the church? A lot. The struggles of parishes with Hispanic ministry

[13] See Hosffman Ospino, *Hispanic Ministry in Catholic Parishes*, 34. See also Hosffman Ospino and Patricia Weitzel-O'Neill, *Catholic Schools in an Increasingly Hispanic Church: A Summary Report of Findings from the National Survey of Catholic Schools Serving Hispanic Families* (Huntington, IN: Our Sunday Visitor), 2016.

often translate into mergers, closings, and fewer resources to advance ministry with this population. Dioceses in the South and the West, where the Hispanic population has grown exponentially, do not have enough resources to build new parishes, centers, and schools to meet the pastoral needs of this population. Neither do they have the personnel to work with them. The lack of a robust presence of pastoral leaders to work with Hispanic Catholics in our ecclesial and academic structures leads to the making of decisions that seldom have the actual needs of this group in mind. Without adequate levels of school completion and ministerial training, these voices will continue to be absent from the table. The needs of Hispanic youth are far from being met. Many young Hispanics do not see the church as their home anymore, even when their parents and grandparents hold on to a faith that is deeply ingrained into their culture. But young Hispanics are now part of a new culture: the United States. About one in four Hispanics in the United States is a former Catholic (about 14 million), most under the age of twenty-four and US born. They have drifted away.

Are US Catholics, Hispanic and non-Hispanic, particularly those in charge of the venues and platforms that amplify the voices of the polarized extremes in the church, aware of these realities? Perhaps. Do they care to address them as priorities? Do they find the passion to make them their own? There is little evidence that such is the case. Most Catholic newspapers, magazines, books, and media expressions in the United States seldom focus on the just-described realities that are directly impacting the lives of Hispanic Catholics in our country. When they do, they do it in passing, sporadically, often without much depth and with little response. These are not the hot-button issues that galvanize liberal and conservative constituencies. They don't arouse the passions and the energy of the polarized margins. Perhaps these margins are already too far removed from the unheeded middle. But for those who live in that middle, which happens to be largely Hispanic, these realities are vital and personal. They are about enduring the daily struggle . . . staying alive . . . keeping the faith . . . waiting in hope . . . living with dignity . . . celebrating the smallest achievement.

A Chance to Be Truly Catholic

Twenty years ago, US Hispanic theologian Allan Figueroa Deck, SJ, wrote an essay with a similar focus to the one in this chapter.[14] In his essay, Figueroa Deck observed that the polarized approaches that tend to dominate Catholic conversations in the United States often ignore the Hispanic experience. As indicated above, this has not changed much. In his analysis, he proposed that Hispanic Catholicism be embraced as "a test case and a bridge between the official Catholicism of the West (of which mainstream US Roman Catholicism is a notable expression) and the many 'local' Catholicisms that fall outside that mainstream."[15] His argument relies on the hope that Catholics are able to transcend divisive polarizations, often influenced by particular political agendas and the rationalistic individualism introduced by Modernism, retrieving a Catholic imagination that builds on the power of polyvalent symbols and the primacy of community. Much in the Hispanic religious and cultural worldview is imbued precisely by such perspectives. So is the worldview of many other groups that constitute the church in the United States. The possibilities are many.

Figueroa Deck proposes a valid alternative to polarization that can help us be creatively Catholic. In that sense I want to echo it. Such an approach is a reminder of the profound ecclesial, spiritual, and pastoral spirit that has prevailed in the life of the church since early Christianity. Are US Catholics ready and

---

[14] Allan Figueroa Deck, "'A Pox on Both Your Houses': A View of Catholic Conservative-Liberal Polarities from the Hispanic Margin," in *Being Right: Conservative Catholics in America*, ed. Mary Jo Weaver and R. Scott Appleby (Bloomington, IN: Indiana University Press, 1995), 88–104.

[15] Ibid., 92.

willing to accept it? Are we open to finding life and a common ecclesial vision in a middle that is enriched by healthy tension yet does not dissolve in extremes? My sense is that as long as we continue to ignore those voices and experiences in the life of the church that embody versions of such an alternative, extreme polarization will continue to win the day. Hispanic Catholicism is no longer a marginal experience in the United States—and it should not be seen as such.

Whether most Hispanics, particularly young US-born Hispanics, will remain Catholic is part of the challenge that the church in the United States needs to confront as we move along into this early part of the twenty-first century. Not long ago, the Catholic bishops of the United States, reflecting on what Hispanic Catholics represent for Catholicism, recognized this same challenge. In their own words:

> The Hispanic presence is also a prophetic warning to the Church in the United States. For if Hispanic Catholics are not welcomed warmly and offered a home where they can experience our Church as their Church, the resulting loss of their Catholic identity will be a serious blow to the Church in our country. We will have missed an opportunity to be truly Catholic.[16]

This seems the appropriate time to return to that first personal experience shared at the beginning of this chapter, when I was formally confronted with the idea of polarization as a young Hispanic student of theology. Two decades later, I continue to grow in the understanding of my faith and what it means to be Catholic in the United States. I am more familiar with the debates, categories, and nuances about polarization that permeate much of our conversations. As an academic, I am constantly engaged in good interchanges, often requiring critical argumentation and even some positioning. As a pastoral

---

[16] National Conference of Catholic Bishops, *The Hispanic Presence in the New Evangelization in the United States* (Washington, DC: USCCB, 1996), 31.

leader, I have grown more sensitive to how fast I can journey with my fellow sisters and brothers on matters perceived as polarizing: when to rest, when to push, how much to question.

I am happy to share that I very much continue to "stand with the Christian tradition" discerned with the people of God in the United States, a community increasingly Hispanic, inserted in the sociohistorical context of American Catholicism. I am a few years older. I have invested much of my life into this American Catholic experience as a Hispanic theologian and made clear commitments to my faith community as a pastoral leader. I am also mindful that the vast majority of young US Catholics, Hispanic and non-Hispanic, as well as the new immigrants in the church, will likely not follow such a path. But it gives me hope that, while the polarized margins sail further apart from the unheeded middle, many Catholics in that middle still linger, extraordinarily waiting to be engaged in ways that resonate with their joys and hopes, griefs and anxieties. We must hurry. They might not wait too long.

13
Can the Church Transcend a Polarized Culture?

Michael Peppard

Polarized American Culture

Scholars agree that the United States has become increasingly polarized over the past forty years. Analyzing the possible causes has become a hot topic for peer-reviewed scholarship, op-ed pages, blogs, and classroom arguments. Was polarization catalyzed by *Roe v. Wade* or *Bush v. Gore*? Do we blame the rise of Rush Limbaugh's "rage radio" or CNN's erstwhile *Crossfire*? Or are cultural touchstones like these just symptoms of other hard to detect pathogens, the real causes hidden below the surface of our body politic? In any case, it's hard to remember the map before it showed red and blue states.

Political scientists and sociologists have been wielding scalpels and microscopes in search of the pathogens affecting our civic bloodstream. Here's a summary of some key findings.[1] Robert Putnam and David Campbell's book *American Grace: How Religion Divides Us and Unites Us* tells the recent history of religion and politics by charting a cultural "shock"—the

---

[1] See John Sides and Daniel J. Hopkins, eds., *Political Polarization in American Politics* (New York: Bloomsbury USA, 2015).

long 1960s—and two "aftershocks."[2] The sexual revolution, coupled with a perfect storm of Supreme Court cases about religion in public schools and abortion, jolted the tectonic plates that undergirded religious identity in the United States. This led to, first, the rise of the Religious Right and, as a response to the Religious Right, the subsequent disaffection by others from organized religion (the rise of the "nones"). These aftershocks have led to a reconfiguration of alliances, such that political affiliation is no longer driven by denomination but by devotion, no longer by religious affiliation but by *religiosity*. For example, when measuring the intensity of religiosity in sociological terms (attendance at services, frequency of prayer, etc.), current Democrats significantly trail the overall demographics. Other political scientists isolate *race* as a primary cause, citing how current Republican adherents significantly trail overall demographics in terms of ethnic diversity. While the race and religiosity arguments track a decades-long shift, many would add a more recent change—the rapidly increasing acceptance of *homosexuality*—to the mix of factors affecting polarization.

Quantitative analyses show that the last twenty years of elections have been extremely competitive (i.e., close margins of victory), and so it is not surprising that the electorate feels more polarized. The mere fact of evenly matched opponents, whether in sports or politics, generates "rah-rah" partisanship. But perhaps polarization is just another word for *well sorted*. Are we more polarized than before, or rather sorting ourselves more effectively, as scholars have shown, through *local migrations* based on income, education, marital status, and other indicators of *assortative mating*? State legislatures respond to local migrations by *gerrymandering* "safe districts" of like-minded citizens, while *activist organizations*, *lobbyists*, and *marketing gurus* fashion ways to bolster the ideological boundaries of sorted groups into *targetable microcultures*. The

---

[2] Robert D. Putnam and David E. Campbell, *American Grace: How Religion Divides and Unites Us* (New York: Simon and Schuster, 2010), especially chap. 4.

well-sorted and ideologically pure respond well to *culture war rhetoric*, which is offered in heavy doses by potent advocacy organizations, such as Planned Parenthood and the National Rifle Association.

The increasingly partisan "old media" of *cable news* and *talk radio* help to further segment the population by stimulating the primordial parts of our brain that derive pleasure from *tribalism*. Neurological studies of extreme partisans have shown that media consumption within an "echo chamber" of one's own opinions may be literally, physiologically *addictive*. Analyses of the media's role in polarization have found a corresponding result, however, that may give a glimmer of hope: partisan media do produce extreme segments that are more fired up than ever, but they also lead to *a more moderate core* that is turned off by polarization. That is to say, current media offerings do not increase the quantity of partisans, but their intensity—*affective polarization*, or dislike for the other party. The rise of "new media" or *social media* then offers a savvy way to compound the effects of sorting, lobbying, and marketing on a group's affective polarization. When presented with either challenging facts and perspectives that provoke cognitive dissonance or an emotive piece of "click bait" in perfect tune with one's chosen echo chamber, most people prefer to follow their instincts toward tribalistic pleasure. Who wouldn't want his "righteous mind," in the words of Jonathan Haidt's influential book, to be continually assured of its rightness as often as possible?[3]

That sums up about twelve different causes of polarization identified by scholars in recent years. Which of these are affecting the church?

What Does a Polarized Culture Have to Do with the Church?

Almost all these features of the body politic can be found in the body of Christ. Sociologists Putnam and Campbell show

---

[3] Jonathan Haidt, *The Righteous Mind: Why Good People Are Divided by Politics and Religion* (New York: Vintage Books, 2012).

that Catholics were not insulated from the "shock and two after-shocks" of the past fifty years. In fact, Peter Steinfels's book, *A People Adrift: The Crisis of the Roman Catholic Church in America*, reads like a companion volume to the sociologists' general take on American religion, with the Catholic version highlighting *Humanae Vitae, Roe v. Wade*, and the sexual abuse scandals as crises of authority that led to polarization.[4] Watching Protestant denominations proceed with ordaining women has also fueled some Catholics' polarized attitudes on issues related to priestly ordination. With regard to race, Catholics are actually among the most integrated religions in America, especially in urban parishes, but vignettes from around the country nonetheless narrate tensions that arise from quick demographic change. When an Oklahoma parish changes from predominantly Polish to predominantly Mexican in half a generation, for instance, not everyone gets along. Even if the two ethnic groups have good will toward one another, it is the rare person that loves in equal measure both a Polka Mass and a Mariachi Mass.

Regarding our rapid cultural shift with respect to homo-sexuality—arguably the fastest change on a major moral issue in the history of our country—Catholics have thus far mapped on to the rest of the country. That is, Catholics are divided by generation on this issue in ways not really distinguishable from overall opinion. But when sociologists take the intensity of Catholic religiosity into account, a further fragmentation appears: Catholics, Evangelicals, and Mormons with high indexes of religiosity have banded together to make common cause against the mainstreaming of homosexuality and same-sex marriage (as with "The Manhattan Declaration" or opposition to Proposition 8 in California).

Catholics have also sorted themselves in different ways than prior eras. Whereas previous generations had either "territorial" parishes (with boundaries by neighborhood) or "national"

---

[4] Peter Steinfels, *A People Adrift: The Crisis of the Roman Catholic Church in America* (New York: Simon and Schuster, 2003).

parishes (typically gathered around a common language), recent years have seen the rise of what we might call "ideological" parishes. Just as citizens have sorted themselves through local migrations into enclaves of the like-minded, so do some Catholics seek out parishes that emphasize their preferred aspects of Catholicism. Most of us can picture a parish nearby that gives off a conservative or a liberal vibe, whether in terms of music, vestments, the prayers of the faithful, homilies, youth group activities, advocacy organizations, or what Catholic periodicals are available in the narthex.

When Catholics occupy such "safe districts" (to borrow a phrase from political culture), they feel less challenged by teachings or people that make them uncomfortable. They are assured of their rightness and, if unchecked, such parishes are fertile soil for self-righteousness. In my home state of Colorado, for instance, I have attended a parish that did not mention the plight of migrants once in a year and offered nothing in Spanish, while only ten miles away another parish did not mention abortion once in a year. Although Catholics do always encounter Jesus during the Liturgy of the Eucharist, if the moral perspectives of parishioners are never challenged during the Liturgy of the Word, the fullness of Jesus' message is not being manifested.

Nor has Catholic media been immune to American polarization. Our media—mostly print and web journalism, with a few prominent video outlets—have struggled to stay afloat since the recession that slashed-and-burned newspapers and magazines across the country. Almost every outlet that has survived did so by holding a niche audience and catering to its interests and opinions. The number of writers contributing to both the *National Catholic Register* and *National Catholic Reporter* is slim to none; the number of readers prayerfully considering the position statements of both Call to Action and the Cardinal Newman Society is probably zero. In the case of advocacy organizations fueled by the captive audience of "choose your own media," the war rhetoric of political culture has infiltrated the church. According to political scientist Sean Theriault, "[T]he warfare dimension taps into the strategies that go beyond defeating your opponents to humiliating them, go beyond questioning your opponents' judgment to questioning their motives, and go beyond fighting the good . . . fight to destroying the institution and the [. . .] process."[5]

At the same time, the fact that Catholics are willing to fight each other openly, airing our dirty laundry, is paradoxically a sign of Catholicism's general acceptance—even dominance—in contemporary America. Smaller religious groups, such as the Eastern Orthodox in the United States, prefer to keep their ideological struggles as invisible as possible to outsiders so as not to threaten the boundaries of their identity. Catholics, on the other hand, have a sitting vice president, seven of the last ten Speakers of the House, and a pope that is verifiably the most popular person on the planet. Six of the nine members of the Supreme Court identify with Catholicism in some way, and every few months, we get to watch them disagree in public. Catholics are polarized, in part, because we have been so successfully integrated into American culture, for better and worse. How can we retain the goodness of America—liberty, diversity, religiosity—without becoming further polarized? How can we avoid having red and blue parishes?

Proposals for Rising above the Partisan Battlefield

Catholics can learn to transcend our polarized American culture, but it will not be easy and will be frequently uncomfortable. While we cannot fully escape these cultural forces (at least not without becoming sectarian, like the Amish), there are a few ways that the church can try to rise above them. The following proposals emphasize four areas of church life. First,

---

[5] Sean Theriault, "Partisan Warfare Is the Problem," in *Political Polarization in American Politics*, ed. John Sides and Daniel J. Hopkins (New York: Bloomsbury USA, 2015), 11.

let us begin where the Common Ground Initiative statement concluded: "Ultimately, the fresh eyes and changed hearts we need . . . emerge in the space created by praise and worship. The revitalized Catholic common ground will be marked by a determined pastoral effort to keep the liturgy, above all, from becoming a battleground for confrontation and polarization."[6]

In the realm of liturgy, a space uniquely suited to cultivate experiences of transcendence, Catholic pastors and lay leaders should curate a unity-in-diversity. For example, music ministers can draw widely and deeply from the Catholic traditions of the parish, making sure to retain treasures such as the seasonal Marian chants, while welcoming the best of the new. In terms of prayers, pastoral associates can take great care with the prayers of the faithful, which literally put words in our mouths and direct them to God. As a rule of thumb, a visitor should not be able to tell the political voting patterns of a parish by listening to the prayers read from the pulpit. Homilists can select their topics and saintly examples from a broad range of issues and historical figures, even laboring to lift up for recognition representatives of the church that have felt marginalized. Pope Francis, during his pastoral visit to the United States, offered a great model for doing so, when he continued to highlight saintly American Catholic women during his speeches: St. Katharine Drexel, St. Elizabeth Ann Seton, Dorothy Day, and more. Finally, Bishop Daniel Flores reminds us that we cannot rely on the Mass alone to do the work of liturgical identity formation; many Latino communities exhibit a robust sacramental, communal life of festivals, pilgrimages, parades, and dramatizations that foster community independent of priestly leadership and opposed to partisan squabbles. We don't necessarily need to roll large wheels of fire down hillsides on the feast of St. John the Baptist, as Europeans once

---

[6] Common Ground Initiative, *Called to Be Catholic*, section 4, http://www .catholiccommonground.org/called-be-catholic.

did, but festive communal gatherings in quasi-public spaces would help to rekindle the spark of distinctive Catholic identity.

Second, in the realm of moral issues, Catholic leaders should commit to disrupting typical partisan divisions by juxtaposing topics that are usually opposed in our political culture. The bishops themselves have set a great example on this. Every partisan should be made uncomfortable by some aspect of their document, *Forming Consciences for Faithful Citizenship*. More recently, the Ad Hoc Committee on Religious Liberty juxtaposed its opposition to the "HHS Mandate" (requiring contraception to be part of insurance plans under the Affordable Care Act) with opposition to anti-immigration laws in border states, which attempted to criminalize the "harboring" of undocumented immigrants (thus making many Catholic pastors *de facto* guilty of crime for exercising charity and hospitality). At the local level, simple ecclesial decisions can send a big message. For example, the diocese of Camden (New Jersey) has an Office of Life & Justice Ministries, which builds the Catholic consistent ethic of life into the administrative structure of the church. Catholics drawn there for one kind of advocacy will meet others that have opposite political leanings. But they are united by what Camden's office calls "the ampersand"—the "&" that bonds human life to social justice. As Cardinal Timothy Dolan said in a speech before Barack Obama and John McCain, Catholics "are called to care for the 'uns': the *un*-employed; the *un*-insured; the *un*-wanted; the *un*-wed mother, and her innocent, fragile *un*-born baby in her womb; the *un*-documented; the *un*-housed; the *un*-healthy; the *un*-fed; the *under*-educated."[7] The Gospel of the "&" is the Gospel of the "uns." Down in his diocese of Brownsville, Texas, Bishop Flores asks pro-life activists and immigration activists to work together—or at least meet together. The "social contact theory" of sociology shows that the most effective way to

[7] Timothy Dolan, "Remarks at 67th Annual Alfred E. Smith Memorial Foundation Dinner," October 18, 2012, http://cardinaldolan.org/index.php /al-smith-foundation-dinner-2/.

eliminate prejudice and polarization is consistent, face-to-face meeting over time between community members of the same relative social status. Whenever Catholic leaders bring together those who care for the unborn with those who care for the undocumented, stewardship of creation with stewardship of religious liberty, or criticism of Planned Parenthood with criticism of the National Rifle Association, they exemplify how Catholic moral theology and social thought does not fit neatly into the political culture of the United States.

Third, in all facets of church life, we can create spaces for graced encounters across lines of language and color. All of us can work harder to diversify the parish, which is, after all, a multicultural mission delivered directly by the Holy Spirit at Pentecost. If a multilingual liturgy or multilingual parent meeting about First Communion strikes you as annoying, just remember that's the Holy Spirit annoying you—with a reminder of the necessity of our linguistic and ethnic diversity. Would it be more efficient to divide up all the liturgies and meetings into English-only or Spanish-only or Tagalog-only? Of course. But the communal and spiritual benefits gained by occasional, well-crafted, multilingual parish events are worth the extra time. Feast days and holy days are especially well-suited to this. Invite a parishioner to explain why *Nuestra Señora de Guadalupe* is such a central figure to Mexicans and another to tell the story of devotion to the Infant Jesus of Prague in Eastern Europe. Are you worried people won't attend a celebration of the other ethnicity's saint? Have all the kids learn each other's songs and perform together—the parents will certainly come. The spiritual rewards of multilingual and multiethnic parish events are difficult to quantify, but one thing is sure: through social contact, such events build goodwill and lessen the temptations toward self-righteousness.

Finally, Catholics tempted toward one end of a polarized American spectrum can commit to diversifying their media intake. This recommendation won't affect everyone equally, since many Catholics consume little to no media about the church (unless the pope visits!). But for those of us who are high consumers of media, we live in a paradoxical moment: it has never been easier to access a wide diversity of media but never more tempting to remain in a partisan echo chamber. On the one hand, the explosion of the Internet in the past ten years has eroded a sense of institutional authority over information and thereby democratized journalism. News outlets that didn't exist two years ago have become major sources of information and analysis. And through a constantly updating stream of news to a pocket portal, one can follow the activities of the church across the globe in real time. On the other hand, no one will curate your newsfeed for you with the goal of juxtaposing seemingly polarized opposites. Our natural inclinations are to seek out sources that tell us what we want to hear, and media companies (with their data algorithms analyzing our "likes" and "favorites") will further target us with information and opinions that keep us affixed to the screen—and "liking" it all. Each of us has the responsibility to diversify our own newsfeed, like a balanced diet, so that we consume reasoned and representative reporting on the church and the world. When we do that, the experience is discomforting but, ultimately, enriching.

In addition, our lives should be interspersed with significant Sabbaths from media saturation. To reorient ourselves to the sacramental encounter with other humans, we should take to heart the claim of theologian Christopher Pramuk about "media supremacy," which is

> a public and increasingly private atmosphere of imagery and language so rancorously divisive and often violent with respect to difference that it threatens to bury our most basic capacities for empathy, intimacy, and love beneath an avalanche of narcissism, political self-interest, and distraction. All of which add up to a very different kind of presence and power at work in our relational lives and shaping our conception of the real at every level.[8]

---

[8] Christopher Pramuk, *Hope Sings, So Beautiful: Graced Encounters across the Color Line* (Collegeville, MN: Liturgical Press, 2013), 132.

So yes, by all means add a *First Things* subscription alongside your *Commonweal*. Or next time the pope makes the news, watch some Chris Matthews alongside EWTN. But more importantly, turn it all off sometimes. Find that family you used to see at church but don't anymore. Find out why they left. And invite them back. The church, at its best, has the Gospel, the Eucharist, the hymns, the saints, and the most diverse membership of any institution on earth. Our media sound bites are often noisy gongs and clanging cymbals, drowning out the sound of the Spirit and the cry of the poor. In the words of Pope Francis, we must promote a "culture of encounter."

When We Fail to Transcend

All of this is difficult—from learning unfamiliar songs and saints, to reorienting our moral spheres, to bumbling uncomfortably in other languages, to reading opinions that strike us as plain wrong. It is far easier to stay on one's home turf, where things make sense. The world has precious few imitators of Socrates, wandering the marketplace, looking for someone to tell them they're missing some key aspect of life. We are hardwired to seek out stimuli that accord with our preconceptions, especially if they solidify our membership in a group. To address the problem of polarization, then, we have to transcend not only our culture but also our human nature.

Can the church deal with a problem both natural and cultural? At its best, the church is perfectly suited to the task. Through liturgy, Scripture, and the traditions of Catholic Social Thought, we are called to prophetically resist the body politic when it harms the Body of Christ. And we have many examples, both scriptural and saintly, of a self-mastery that rejects the sinful tug of human nature toward tribalism.

Even so, we will frequently fail to transcend our differences. Even as I write this, I'm skeptical of my own proposals. Are calls for transcending polarization hopelessly naïve, as late church historian Richard McBrien had lamented? That's possible, since we've been divided on key issues from the beginning, like when Paul got in Peter's face at Antioch about a foundational matter (Gal 2:11). Paul had the notion—naïve, even crazy—that God had opened up the covenant to Gentiles. But we might take Peter's response in this encounter as a model: it is acceptable, even essential, to challenge one another on weighty matters but not advisable to deny another's Christian identity. Peter and others may have challenged Paul's apostleship but not his discipleship. There is a profound difference between Peter saying, "Paul, are you sure that's what God is calling us to do?" and "Paul, you are not a Christian." Despite their confrontation in Antioch, our tradition holds that these two culture warriors met again in Rome, where they found their unity-in-diversity. Church history proves that the line between naïveté and hope is not always clear.

When we feel ourselves failing, we might use the early Christian era to think with. When we worry about factiousness, we can recall the major disagreements in Corinth that led to Paul's "one body, many parts" teaching. When we worry about overheated rhetoric, we can recall that Jesus called Peter "Satan" at a moment of exasperation, and that there were physical fights at ancient church councils. When we worry about ideological sorting, we can recall that the early church in Syria had different emphases in ritual, prayer, music, ecclesiastical offices, and theology than Christians in Rome or Egypt. Yet these diverse "parishes," if you will, found a way to carry the message of Jesus and the traditions of the apostles forward through the years, across boundaries of language, culture, and theology.

Sometimes we may have to imitate how the apostles dealt with differences: dividing up turf or choosing different types of mission, then meeting together for discussion of successes and failures, forgiving each other before approaching the altar and always remembering to break bread together and serve the poor. Even if we fail to transcend our differences, an imitation of such a model is a kind of apostolic succession.

I conclude with a snapshot of my parish, from a Sunday in April 2015 that captures some of the graced juxtapositions I have in mind. This is the parish that left me stunned my first day there by praying for the unborn and the undocumented, by praying for those suffering in Iraq and also the safety of our military, by weaving Spanish and English prayers together in an oblation worthy of God. On this day, Mass proceeded more or less normally, except that we were hosting a relic of John Paul II, who had been recognized as a saint the previous year. Communion had been distributed, the prayers concluded, and the pastor stood for the week's announcements. Some were typical: a trivia night fundraiser for the school, a mission trip to the Dominican Republic, a book discussion group. Amid these, listed as any other announcement, was the monthly gay fellowship, to which all were welcome. And at the end, the pastor invited up a parishioner, let's call her Paula, for a special announcement. This Latina lawyer in her late twenties, a devout member of the church, gave a short testimony that she would soon be entering religious life as a nun. She recounted the support of the parish, from her youth to the present, in cultivating her vocation. Now she needed help to pay her law school loans and hoped the church could play a role. Why is this so shocking, that a parish with a gay fellowship also cultivates vocations to consecrated religious life? It shouldn't be. It's a snapshot of a "here comes everybody" kind of Catholic Church, embodying a catholicity that is, in the words of Cardinal Bernardin, "both a tradition and a dream to be handed on."

I should say what happened next. We stood for the recessional hymn, which was the Regina Caeli chant. In Latin. Everyone sang. And as we were finishing, the side door opened, through which an elderly Latino guitarist began to roll in his equipment, to get ready for the Spanish Mass. The recessional spilled onto the street, where our English-speaking kids crowded the table of fresh *pastelitos* for sale. Here comes everybody—do we welcome them?

Conclusion

Resisting Polarization: Naming a Moment of Hope

Charles C. Camosy

This book has presented us with several important insights about polarization. I've learned much from listening to contributors at the Notre Dame conference and then reading their expanded thoughts for this volume. I've also learned about polarization from several other events and projects with which I've been involved. Doing public bioethics as a Roman Catholic theologian, by the very nature of the enterprise, means dealing head-on with polarization.[1] In addition to right/left political polarization within the American Catholic Church, I've thought and written quite a bit on religious/secular polarization—particularly when it comes to a person many believe to be the most polarizing figure of all in (bio)ethics, Peter Singer.[2] I've also had an intense focus on the polarization found in

---

[1] Indeed, precisely because of these political pressures, the last decade has seen Catholic moral theologians refuse to specialize in bioethics—with the result that there are almost no Catholic doctoral programs in theology currently in a position to train students in this field. Thus many bioethics positions go unfilled, and the public discourse on complex yet polarizing issues like abortion, physician-assisted suicide, health care distribution, and more are increasingly disconnected from the moral-theological tradition of the Church.

[2] Charles Camosy, *Peter Singer and Christian Ethics: Beyond Polarization* (Cambridge, UK: Cambridge University Press, 2012).

the American public discourse on abortion. In addition to organizing a major international conference on abortion at Princeton University in 2010, my most recent book is an explicit proposal for thinking and speaking about abortion in a new and nonpolarized way.[3]

On the basis of these and other experiences, I've come to see the most pernicious offenses of polarizations to be of two kinds:

1. *An offense against truth.* Our polarized discourse expects to see only two possible answers to a question. This forces the answer to a complex question (or set of questions) into a lazy, simplistic, binary framework. And in using this framework, one is forced to abandon the truth of the complexity involved in answering some of our culture's most pressing questions.

2. *An offense against charity.* A polarized binary, of its very nature, pits one side against the other side. "Us" versus "them." The other side becomes the enemy against which one is pitted even before the issues are engaged. Indeed, one's identity becomes just as much about one's distaste for and opposition to "the other side" as it is about anything one actually shares with one's own side.[4] Thus, the charity which Christ commanded us to have for our neighbor becomes nearly impossible, without abandoning the very assumptions around which one has built one's identity.

---

[3] Charles Camosy, *Beyond the Abortion Wars: A Way Forward for a New Generation* (Grand Rapids, MI: Eerdmans, 2015).

[4] I've seen this as full display in my study of our public discourse on abortion. People and groups who identity as "pro-choice" or "pro-life" may actually share several important goals in common but nevertheless be unable to work together on such goals because working with "the other side" is just so distasteful for them. Their very identify comes from opposing "the other" people and groups. Working with them in a positive way risks undoing the kind of identity that defines one's self by opposition to another.

When we think about polarization in the US Catholic Church, we often forget to think about sin. We are flawed, fallible, finite beings—prone to the kinds of self-deception and idolatry that make it difficult for us to see that we are actually part of the right/left polarization in the church leading to (1) and (2) above. The neurosciences and social sciences have confirmed that we *Homo sapiens* generally see what we expect or desire to see. It is therefore anything but surprising that so many of us think of ourselves as "moderate" or otherwise not part of the problem. But it is time to face facts: far too often, American Catholics make an idol out of a secular political party or ideology, and in so doing, accept the polarized right/left binary that comes with it. Also far too often, American Catholics sit in echo chambers (in their parishes, neighborhoods, schools, news channels, social media intake, etc.) that do little but confirm the mistaken impressions they have of themselves as being moderate, open-minded, and complex thinkers who are not part of the problem.

Of course, the antagonistic division this creates in the Body of Christ is at anything but the service of the Gospel. As Michael Peppard demonstrated in this volume,[5] it is at the service of politicians and secular political parties, which use the "us versus them" polarized narrative to raise money, mobilize volunteers, and ask for votes. It is also at the service of media organizations who tell a simplistic but entertaining "war" or "battle" narrative that generates ratings and hits. In another life, I studied broadcast journalism, and the first rule of the newsroom we learned was, "If it bleeds, it leads." When speaking of public discourse, this means that virtually all debates and disagreements are seen through an aggressive and antagonistic lens in which "one side" is attacking "the other side." This is the kind of narrative that makes money for the shareholders of NBC Universal, Newscorp, Turner Broadcast-

---

[5] See Michael Peppard in chap. 13 of this volume, p. 145.

ing, and the other corporations that serve as the gatekeepers of our public discourse.

How Can We Resist Polarization?

Despite the deep and profound interest of the corporate/media/political/industrial complex keeping everyone, including the American Catholic Church, trapped in a right/left binary imagination, this book has provided many important ways for us to resist. Indeed, I would argue that the ideas presented in this book—coupled with the historical moment in which they are offered—constitute a singular and powerful moment of hope that things can be done differently. But we would do well to take advantage of this moment with specific plans and goals—plans and goals to which we are committed, with the kind of intentionality and energy that can resist the powerful cultural forces pushing us in a very different direction. Building on the work of my colleagues in this book, here are some ideas.

Picking up on the important message of the Focolare community, our first commitment must be to live as a church that intentionally thinks of unity with a trinitarian imagination.[6] That is, we shouldn't be thinking of our unity as somehow distinct from our diversity. Though always bounded and binded by the church, we must be committed to genuine (not token) diversity of relationships and viewpoints within our communities. These kinds of communities are required if we are to resist the limitations of our sinful natures and the tendency to deceive ourselves into seeing what we expect or desire to see. We must have people in our close orbit who think differently from us and who have permission to challenge our point of view.

Bishops ought to be advised by a diverse team who sometimes disagree with their boss—and with each other. Theologians ought to attend conferences where those with very

---

[6] Amy Uelmen and Thomas Masters, *Focolare: Living the Spirituality of Unity in the United States* (New York: New City Press, 2011).

different points of view challenge each other. Faithful Catholics ought to attend Mass and live in communities open to people who think very differently from themselves. Julia Brumbough, one of the special delegates to the conference which led to this book, said in an interview for the conference video that her commitment to diversity means she wants to attend Mass "with people who make my blood boil."[7] This approach helpfully resists the phenomenon of "parish shopping," which Tricia Bruce discusses in her contribution to this book.[8] Instead of seeking out parishes that conform to our many theological, liturgical, and political sensibilities, we ought to be open to attending parishes where our point of view will be genuinely challenged.

Of course, if we are serious about being genuinely challenged, Amy Uelmen reminds us that we must begin by listening.[9] We must see ourselves first as Pope Francis sees himself first: as a sinner. Again, we are prone to mistakes and self-deception, and we ought to reserve the right to change our mind as the result of listening to the insights of someone who thinks differently. Most often, this is neither easy nor pleasant. It doesn't feel good to have our blood boiled by someone with a very different point of view. As the Focolare movement also reminds us, Christ's example demonstrates that this will involve suffering. But the payoff is too important to ignore: as Susan C. Sullivan notes in her piece,[10] truly diverse parishes can actually become centers of resisting polarization.

It is also worth mentioning that actually listening to "the other" can lead to insights about that person that can break apart the polarized binary such that they no longer fit into a

---

[7] Notre Dame Conference, "Polarization in the American Catholic Church," YouTube, posted September 15, 2015, https://www.youtube.com /watch?v = yDmpWp_X7o0.

[8] See Tricia Bruce in chap. 3 of this volume, p. 33.

[9] See Amy Uelmen in chap. 8 of this volume, p. 88.

[10] See Susan Crawford Sullivan in chap. 4 of this volume, p. 46.

nice, clean, and dismissible box. I've been fortunate enough to have several such experiences. In dialoguing with a committed and actively gay Catholic man, for instance, I found that—despite his disagreeing with the institutional church on some matters—he nevertheless had a very traditional commitment to the liturgical norms of the Mass and even got annoyed when priests deviated from those norms. I've also dialogued with a pro-life woman whom I knew regularly prayed outside abortion clinics, attended the March for Life every year, and only voted on abortion around election time—but whom I came to learn also founded and ran her parish soup kitchen and homeless shelter. David Gushee tells in this volume his story of being raised Catholic in the 1970s and—from his perspective as someone with deeply held, left-leaning social justice concerns—leaving the church because he just couldn't take the post–Vatican II catechesis he was getting seriously.[11] Genuinely listening to those outside our camp can open us to complex and interesting stories that challenge conventional, polarized, binary wisdom.

The difficulty inherent in this kind of listening, however, requires cultivating the virtue of solidarity. In this context, solidarity involves an active (rather than passive) listening, expecting that one has something to learn, making genuine attempts to understand the factors that led someone to their position, and addressing the most persuasive version of their position. This kind of solidarity means never reducing another's ideas to their gender, race, level of privilege, sexual orientation, or social location. It means never dismissing them on the basis of what you suspect are their "secret personal motivations"—a practice that is often returned in kind and blows up genuine engagement.

[11] See David P. Gushee in chap. 7 of this volume, p. 79.

On Not Papering Over Our Differences

But what happens when we move beyond the listening stage, actually begin to engage one another, and inevitably run into serious disagreement? Some may think of what I'm advocating as a kind of "nicey-nice" approach which irresponsibly papers over our differences. But as Holly Taylor Coolman shows in her contribution, this couldn't be further from the truth.[12] Disagreement and argument, if it is to be authentic, must be preceded by the kind of solidarity we just discussed. A polarized relationship precludes authentic disagreement and argument precisely because the positions of one's opponents are either (1) dismissed without argument, or (2) caricatured as hopelessly simplistic. Far from papering over difference, solidarity with one's opponent is what makes an authentic argument possible.

And if our conversation partners are committed to the principle that we are flawed, finite, sinful people—reserving the right to change their minds in light of the engagement—this creates the conditions for firm and even aggressive critique of one's opponent. Inconsistency and hypocrisy left unchecked can lead to injustice. Jesus himself gave us a model for expressing the prophetic nature of discipleship, particularly when it came to his strong criticism of the hypocritical scholars of the law. Sometimes it takes an aggressive approach to give due weight to justice issues at stake in the conversation and to break through ingrained cultural assumptions. We must be careful, however, about aspiring to the biting level of critique Jesus had for his opponents. We are not God. Prone to sinful excess, we risk going too far in making an aggressive critique, breaking the bonds of charity with each other and undermining the very engagement we seek. Prudence requires keeping this squarely in mind when we venture into the waters of aggressive and prophetic critique.

---

[12] See Holly Taylor Coolman in chap. 6 of this volume, p. 69.

One way we can mitigate against this concern is by taking the advice of Michael Sean Winters: make the time to get to know our opponents personally.[13] Especially in a context of impersonal online interaction via blogs and social media, it is too easy for aggressive disagreement to spill over into sinful excess. But sitting across the table from someone, in their physical presence, reminds us not only that our words are directed at real people with real feelings but also that these people have stories and circumstances that we may never discover without such a meeting. Again, human beings most often see what they expect to see. Sometimes it takes being confronted with the objective reality in front of our faces to see something we were not expecting.

Another benefit of making time for personal, embodied interaction is that, as Julie Rubio points out in this book, it can actually lead to surprising areas of common ground and even common cause.[14] This has certainly been my experience with engaging Peter Singer. We firmly and aggressively disagree about the dignity of human life, but after several personal conversations, we found that we could work together on other issues. This led, for example, to a copresentation at the offices of the Humane Society of the United States.[15] Remarkably, in this presentation Singer admitted he was wrong to blame Christian theology for how terribly we treat nonhuman animals and that he now believes Christians and other religious believers can be allies in the struggle to reform our practices in this regard.

This was also my experience with the 2010 abortion conference at Princeton. There, I met a strong abortion rights activist—a person with whom I had very serious and even

[13] See Michael Sean Winters's reflection in chap. 1 of this volume, p. 21.

[14] See Julie Hanlon Rubio's reflection in chap. 1 of this volume, p.11.

[15] The *New York Times* actually did a story which discussed the presentation. Mark Oppenheimer, "Scholars Explore Perspectives on Animal Rights," *New York Times*, December 6, 2013, http://www.nytimes.com/2013/12/07 /us/exploring-christian-perspectives-on-animal-rights.html?_r = 0.

passionate disagreement—but our personal connection led to more discussions about where we shared overlapping concerns. This in turn led to several pro-life Catholic moral theologians joining her amicus brief denouncing laws that mandated the shackling of pregnant, undocumented immigrants. It turns out that when we resist the "us vs. them" polarized framework, the very enemies we imagine we must fight to the death can turn out to be our most powerful allies.

Can we imagine this being the case in the polarized US Catholic Church? Absolutely. In fact, it is already happening in the person of Paul Ryan. Not very long ago, Ryan was firmly planted on the far economic right, touting a kind of Ayn Randian libertarianism when it came to markets and wealth. Several Catholics who identify more with the economic left, however—including John Carr, director of Georgetown University's Initiative on Catholic Social Thought—reached out to Ryan with an invitation to engage the church's teaching on economic justice. The results of this engagement have been profound. Moral and political theologian Matthew Shadle subsequently argued that we "can finally put to rest the accusation that Ryan is really a Randian wolf in sheep's clothing."[16] But let this sink in for moment: if it wasn't for fellow Catholics on the economic left reaching out to Ryan in charity and solidarity, we wouldn't have the current Speaker of the House spearheading what can only be called an unprecedented bipartisan focus on poverty.[17]

Can we do this on a smaller scale in Catholic dioceses and parishes? Absolutely. Suppose parishioners or diocesan staff disagree about the role of government when it comes to being on the side of the least among us. Find other ways to work together. It is an outrage, for instance, that more pro-life

[16] Matthew Shadle, "Paul Ryan's Anti-Poverty Program and Catholic Social Teaching," *Political Theology Today*, August 1, 2014, http://www.politicaltheology .com/blog/paul-ryans-anti-poverty-plan-and-catholic-social-teaching/.

[17] Jake Miller, "Paul Ryan Thrusts Poverty into 2016 Conversation," *CBSNews.com*, January 9, 2016, http://www.cbsnews.com/news/paul -ryan-thrusts-poverty-into-2016-election-conversation/.

ministries do not focus on pregnant women in difficult circumstances. Why can't every parish with the means operate a women's shelter, staffed and supported by people who would otherwise disagree about the government's role in restricting abortion? Why can't every parish with the means operate a drop-in center for the homeless, staffed and supported by people who would otherwise disagree about the government's role in addressing systemic poverty?

As Hosffman Ospino points out in his important piece in this volume, adequately addressing the concerns of the changing demographics of the US Catholic Church means having a focus on issues which are less polarizing.[18] Latino Catholics in the United States are facing desperate struggles with poverty; giving priority to their issues means that the church would quite naturally be in a less polarized situation. A church committed to the well-being of those in desperate circumstances—at the local level, in the trenches—has the additional benefit of being a very attractive community, particularly when it comes to young people. Millennials, though committed to social justice, are increasingly skeptical of big institutions—whether governments, businesses, or national churches. Providing a local, grassroots opportunity to be on the side of the most vulnerable would not only give young people the kind of community that so many of them lack but would also keep them connected to the church. And given the numbers we've seen in this book about the rate at which they are leaving, this is no small thing.

But again, my proposal cannot be reduced to "nicey-nice" cooperation. Though the approaches suggested here will reduce the frequency of intense conflict, there will be many times in which fellow Catholics are compelled by their convictions to work at cross-purposes. In such circumstances, however, let us never forget where our ultimate loyalty lies and how that reality binds us together in ways our disagreements must

---

[18] See Hosffman Ospino in chap. 12 of this volume, p. 130.

never risk tearing apart. Our engagement in the political process must be faithful to Jesus' command to be "in but not of." Again, we must avoid the idolatry of secular, binary, polarized politics—resisting the pressures and strategies of marketing gurus, media pundits, and politicians who want us to play the "us versus them" game. Yes, we should work for the kind of social change demanded by our convictions, and we must be in the world to do this. But we must always remember that the Body of Christ has ultimate loyalty to a kingdom that is not of this world.

Naming a Moment of Hope

Several contributors to this book have highlighted important details about the future of the US Catholic Church. It is clear that we are a church in transition. Christian Smith notes that many young Catholics are *not* polarized, but often this is because they don't know or care enough to have skin in the game.[19] Both Erin Stoyell-Mulholland and Elizabeth Tenety demonstrate that the politics of Millennials—even those who care deeply and are trying to make a difference—are not the politics of the "us versus them" culture wars that have so infected the US church.[20] Indeed, over 50 percent of US Millennials refuse to identify as either Republican or Democrat.[21] Relatedly, Hosffman Ospino shows that the youngest generation of US Catholics is dominated by Latinos—a group whose concerns couldn't be further from the culture wars of the 1970s United States.[22] The questions and debates that gave rise to

[19] See Christian Smith's reflection in chap. 1 of this volume, p. 16.

[20] See Elizabeth Tenety's and Erin Stoyell-Mulholland's work in chaps. 10 and 11 of this volume, pp. 113 and 119.

[21] Amy Sherman, "Half of Millennials Don't Associate with Democrat or Republican Party, Rock the Vote Says," http://www.politifact.com/florida /statements/2014/mar/17/rock-vote/half-millennials-dont-associate -democrat-or-republ/.

[22] See Hosffman Ospino in chap. 12 of this volume, p. 130 .

our current polarized political framework and assumptions just aren't the questions and debates of young Catholics.

As these differently thinking Catholics take their rightful place in the church and the broader culture, we are presented with a great moment of hope. There is every reason to think a new generation is upon us, one that can lead the US church out of our polarized mess. It is a generation which, far from making an idol of belonging to "one side" and opposing "the other side," is highly skeptical of these binary political categories. They want instead to make space for multiple ways of engaging in public discourse and activism. It is a generation more impressed by an ampersand connecting pro-life and social justice concerns than it is by an unfamiliar, polarized 1970s framework that disconnects them. It is a generation which, in short, is far more open to the kind of solidarity necessary to resist polarization.

The demographic changes on the way for US Catholicism are so overwhelming that Millennials may not need the assistance of Generation X or the Baby Boomers in helping the US church to transition out of an idolatrous focus on right/left secular politics. (If they weren't already convinced of this trajectory, the disastrous and even laughable 2016 election cycle has probably done the trick.) Nevertheless, those who hold leadership roles in the church (bishops, pastors, teachers, heads of diocesan offices, etc.) ought to work confidently in creating institutions for the next generation that explicitly reject polarized politics.

There have been several good suggestions along these lines made in this book, but in closing, let me underscore one idea in particular. There is perhaps no more important kind of polarization in the US Catholic Church (and perhaps in our culture more broadly) than between "pro-life Catholics" and "social justice Catholics." The church must energetically resist this kind of polarization by no longer accepting a foreign and artificial divide between the work of pro-life ministries and the work of human concerns or social justice ministries. We must refuse to prioritize one set of concerns over the other set of concerns. We must instead draw people and resources together to see and explain how they are connected—and then move forward together in pushing for social change. The next generation will eventually do this anyway—with or without us—but we would be well-advised to get with the program now.

For those who long for a new kind of politics in the US Catholic Church, there is a moment of hope upon us. Let us work with a new energy to replace polarization with solidarity.

Contributors

Tricia C. Bruce (PhD, University of California, Santa Barbara) is associate professor of sociology at Maryville College and author of *Faithful Revolution: How Voice of the Faithful Is Changing the Church*. Her second book (forthcoming) explores the use of "personal parishes" in response to cultural, ideological, and ethnic diversity among US Catholics. She also coleads the American Parish Project and has conducted applied research for the US Conference of Catholic Bishops.

Charles C. Camosy (PhD, University of Notre Dame) is associate professor of theology at Fordham University. His articles have appeared in publications including *American Journal of Bioethics, Journal of the Catholic Health Association, Los Angeles Times*, and *America*; he is also the author of *Too Expensive to Treat?, Peter Singer and Christian Ethics, For Love of Animals*, and *Beyond the Abortion Wars*. He advises the Faith Outreach office of the Humane Society and the ethics committee of Children's Hospital of New York.

Holly Taylor Coolman is an assistant professor of theology at Providence College (Providence, Rhode Island). Her interests include Thomas Aquinas, theology of law, and theologies of the Jewish people.

Brian P. Flanagan is assistant professor of theology at Marymount University in Arlington, Virginia. His research interests include ecclesiological method, communion ecclesiology, and the work of Jean-Marie Tillard. He wrote *Communion, Diversity, and Salvation: The Contribution of Jean-Marie Tillard to*

Systematic Ecclesiology and has published articles in *Horizons*, *Ecclesiology*, and *Theological Studies* on topics in ecclesiology, interreligious dialogue, and liturgy.

Most Rev. Daniel Flores has served as the bishop of the diocese of Brownsville since 2009. He studied at the University of Dallas and Holy Trinity Seminary and was ordained to the priesthood for the diocese of Corpus Christi. He completed work on a doctoral dissertation in sacred theology at the Angelicum in 2000. Presently, Bishop Flores serves on several USCCB committees and as chair of the Secretariat of Cultural Diversity in the Church.

Nichole M. Flores is assistant professor of religious studies at the University of Virginia (PhD, Boston College). Her research emphasizes the contributions of Catholic and US Latino/a theologies to notions of justice, emotion, and aesthetics as they relate to the common good within plural sociopolitical contexts. Her published work has appeared in the *Journal of the Society of Christian Ethics*, *Feminist Catholic Theological Ethics*, *America* magazine, and the *Washington Post* "On Faith" blog.

David P. Gushee is Distinguished University Professor of Christian Ethics and director of the Center for Theology and Public Life at Mercer University. Widely regarded as one of the leading moral voices in American Christianity, he is the author or editor of twenty books and hundreds of articles in his field, including *Righteous Gentiles of the Holocaust*, *Kingdom Ethics*, *The Sacredness of Human Life*, and, most recently, *Changing Our Mind*. He has lectured on every continent.

Rev. John I. Jenkins, CSC, elected in 2005 as the University of Notre Dame's seventeenth president, has devoted himself to fostering the university's unique place in academia, the church, our nation, and the world. A philosopher trained in theology and a member of Notre Dame's Department of Philosophy since 1990, Fr. Jenkins holds undergraduate and advanced degrees from Notre Dame and a doctorate of philosophy from Oxford University.

Mary Ellen Konieczny is assistant professor of sociology at the University of Notre Dame. She holds a PhD from the University of Chicago and an MDiv from Weston Jesuit School of Theology, and she previously worked in ministry and administration for the Catholic archdiocese of Chicago. Her book, *The Spirit's Tether: Family, Work, and Religion among American Catholics*, is an ethnography of liberal and conservative Catholic parishes, examining how religion and family life support and shape moral and political polarization.

Michael McGillicuddy received his master's degrees in sociology and social work at the University of Illinois at Chicago and his bachelor's degree in theology from Christian Brothers in Memphis. He has worked in financial planning, domestic violence advocacy, and psychiatric social work and cofounded Peaceful Solutions, a consistent ethic initiative based on Cardinal Joseph Bernardin's prophetic message.

Hosffman Ospino (PhD, Boston College) is an assistant professor of theology and religious education at Boston College's School of Theology and Ministry and director of graduate programs in Hispanic ministry. He was the principal investigator for the *National Study of Catholic Parishes with Hispanic Ministry* (2011–2014) and has edited and authored several books on Hispanic ministry, including *Hispanic Ministry in the 21st Century: Present and Future*, and the upcoming *Hispanic Ministry in the 21st Century: Urgent Matters*.

Michael Peppard (PhD, Yale University) is assistant professor of theology at Fordham University. His work brings to light the meanings of early Christian sources in their social, political, artistic, and ritual contexts. His first book, *The Son of God in the Roman World*, received the 2013 Manfred Lautenschläger Award for Theological Promise (University of Heidelberg); more than a dozen scholarly journals have featured Dr. Peppard's articles. He frequently offers commentary in venues such as *Commonweal*, the *New York Times*, the *Washington Post*, PBS, NPR, and CNN.

Julie Hanlon Rubio is professor of Christian ethics at St. Louis University. Her research brings together Catholic Social Teaching and Christian theology on marriage and family. Her articles have appeared in *Theological Studies*, the *Journal of the Society of Christian Ethics*, *Horizons*, INTAMS, the *Journal of Political Theology*, and *Josephinum*. She is the author of *Family Ethics: Practices for Christians*, *A Christian Theology of Marriage and Family*, and *Between the Personal and Political: Catholic Hope for Common Ground*.

Christian Smith (PhD, Harvard University) is the William R. Kenan, Jr. Professor of Sociology at the University of Notre Dame, director of the Center for the Study of Religion and Society, and the principal investigator of the National Study of Youth and Religion, the Science of Generosity Initiative, and the Parenting and the Intergenerational Transmission of Religious Faith Project. Smith is the author, coauthor, or editor of numerous books, including *The Paradox of Generosity*, *The Sacred Project of American Sociology*, *Young Catholic America*, and *Souls in Transition*. Smith's scholarly interests focus on American religion, cultural sociology, adolescents, generosity, sociological theory, and philosophy of social science.

Erin Stoyell-Mulholland studied theology at the University of Notre Dame, during which time she was a Sorin Fellow at the Center for Ethics and Culture, resident assistant in Lewis Hall, and president of Notre Dame Right to Life. She currently works for Students for Life of Illinois doing donor development.

Susan Crawford Sullivan (PhD, Harvard University) is an associate professor of sociology at the College of the Holy Cross. Her research interests focus on sociology of religion, poverty, and family. She has published numerous articles and two books: *A Vision of Justice: Engaging Catholic Social Teaching on the College Campus* and *Living Faith: Everyday Religion and Mothers in Poverty*, winner of multiple book awards.

Elizabeth Tenety has written and edited for *America* magazine and the *Washington Post* and served as editor for the Women & Religion Project at Georgetown University's Berkley Center for Religion, Peace, and World Affairs. She studied theology and government at Georgetown University and received her master's degree in reporting and writing from Northwestern University's Medill School of Journalism.

Amy Uelmen is a lecturer at Georgetown Law School, where her scholarship and teaching focus on the intersection between legal theory, Catholic Social Thought, religious values, and professional life. She was the founding director of Fordham's Institute on Religion, Law, and Lawyer's Work. She holds a BA in American Studies and a JD from Georgetown University, and an MA in theology from Fordham University.

Michael Sean Winters is a columnist at the *National Catholic Reporter*, where his blog "Distinctly Catholic" has won multiple Catholic Press Association Awards. He is the US correspondent for the international Catholic weekly the *Tablet* and a frequent commentator on NPR, PBS, and other media outlets. His books include *Left at the Altar: How the Democrats Lost the Catholics*; *How the Catholics Can Save the Democrats;* and *God's Right Hand: How Jerry Falwell Baptized the American Right and Made God a Republican.*